Does The Bible Ever Contradict Itself?: Demystifying 50 Supposed Inconsistencies

Rev Minton Thomas

Published by Thomas Bika, 2024.

DOES THE BIBLE EVER CONTRADICT ITSELF?: DEMYSTIFYING 50 SUPPOSED INCONSISTENCIES

First edition. April 26, 2024.

ISBN: 979-8224814985

Written by Rev Minton Thomas.

Table of Contents

Preface

WAIT... READ HERE FIRST!

God has revealed his truth to only those who lean unto him for understanding (**Proverbs 3:5-6**). Most people are never able to understand the things of God due to their reliance on worldly knowledge or reason:

1 Corinthians 2:14: states, "The natural person does not accept the things of the Spirit of God, for they are foolishness to him, and he cannot understand them, because they are spiritually discerned." (NIV)

Here, "natural person" refers to someone who relies solely on their own understanding and hasn't received the Holy Spirit. The verse suggests that such a person finds spiritual things foolish because they cannot be grasped through human reason alone.

Matthew 11:25-26: Jesus says in this passage, "At that time Jesus declared, "I thank you, Father, Lord of heaven and earth, that you have hidden these things from the wise and understanding and revealed them to little children. Yes, Father, for this is what you have chosen to do." (NIV)

The scripture speaks of those who are "wise and understanding" – potentially those who rely heavily on intellectual knowledge. Jesus suggests that God reveals his truths to those with a childlike openness and receptivity, not just those with intellectual prowess.

It's important to note that these passages don't imply that education or intelligence are inherently bad. However, they emphasize the importance of a spiritual dimension to understanding God's message. Faith and openness to the Holy Spirit are seen as crucial for grasping spiritual truths.

1 Corinthians 1:18-25 says "For the message of the cross is foolishness to those who are perishing, but to us who are being saved it is the power of God. For it is written: "I will destroy the wisdom of the wise and the intelligence of the intelligent." Where is the wise person? Where is the scholar? Where is the philosopher of this age? Has not God made foolish the wisdom of the world?

For since in the wisdom of God the world through its wisdom did not know God, God was pleased through the foolishness of preaching to save those who believe. For Jews demand signs and Greeks seek wisdom, but we preach Christ crucified, a stumbling block to Jews and foolishness to Gentiles, but to those who are called, both Jews and Greeks, Christ the power of God and the wisdom of God." (NIV):

This passage highlights that God's wisdom isn't always grasped through human logic. Faith plays a crucial role. It for this reason **1 Corinthians 2:14-16** suggests that the natural person does not accept the things of the Spirit of God, for they are foolishness to him, and he cannot understand them, because they are spiritually discerned. The spiritual person judges all things, but no one judges him. "For who has known the mind of the Lord that he may instruct him?" But we have the mind of Christ. (NIV):

Spiritual understanding comes from the Holy Spirit, not just intellectual capacity. James 1:5-8 furthermore says

"If any of you lacks wisdom, you should ask God, who gives generously to all without finding fault, and it will be given to you. But let him ask in faith, having no doubt, for whoever doubts is like a wave of the sea blown and tossed by the wind. That person should not expect to receive anything from the Lord. Such a person is double-minded and unstable in all his ways." (NIV)

Finally at that time Jesus declared, "I thank you, Father, Lord of heaven and earth, that you have hidden these things from the wise and understanding and revealed them to little children. Yes, Father, for this is what you have chosen to do." **Matthew 11:25-26** (NIV):

God reveals himself to those with a humble and open heart, not just those with intellectual pride. He goes on implore us in **Proverbs 3:5-6** Trust in the Lord with all your heart and lean not on your own understanding; in all your ways submit to him, and he will make your paths straight. (NIV)

The Bible itself encourages trusting God and relying on his guidance, not solely on one's own understanding. Remember, God's word is meant to encourage a balance between intellectual pursuit and faith. God's wisdom can be received through both study and a humble heart open to the Holy Spirit.

2 Timothy 3:16 -17

All scripture *is* given by inspiration of God, and *is* profitable for doctrine, for reproof, for correction, for instruction in righteousness:

That the man of God may be perfect, thoroughly furnished unto all good works.

<u>**(King James Version)**</u>

All Scripture is God-breathed and is useful for teaching, rebuking, correcting and training in righteousness,
so that the man of God may be thoroughly equipped for every good work.
<u>**(New International Version)**</u>

All Scripture is inspired by God and is useful to teach us what is true and to make us realize what is wrong in our lives. It straightens us out and teaches us to do what is right.

It is God's way of preparing us in every way, fully equipped for every good thing God wants us to do.
<u>**(New living Version)**</u>

Every part of Scripture is God-breathed and useful one way or another—showing us truth, exposing our rebellion, correcting our mistakes, training us to live God's way.

Through the Word we are put together and shaped up for the tasks God has for us
<u>**(The Message)**</u>

Chapter 1: Introduction

Purpose and Scope of the Book:

The purpose of this book is multifaceted, reflecting a deep commitment to both the integrity of Scripture and the spiritual growth of believers. At its core, the book seeks to provide a comprehensive examination of **50** alleged contradictions in the Bible, aiming to dispel misconceptions and deepen understanding. Through careful analysis and thoughtful reflection, readers are invited into a journey of discovery that illuminates the complex and nuanced nature of Scripture.

The scope of the book is broad, encompassing a wide range of alleged contradictions found throughout the Bible. From apparent inconsistencies in historical accounts to perceived discrepancies in theological teachings, each section delves into a specific contradiction with meticulous attention to detail. By addressing these challenges head-on, the book equips readers with the tools and insights needed to navigate the complexities of Scripture with confidence and clarity.

Scripture itself serves as a guide and inspiration for the purpose and scope of this book. As Psalm 119:105 declares, "Your word is a lamp to my feet and a light to my path." By engaging with alleged contradictions, readers are guided deeper into the truth of God's Word, discovering hidden treasures and gaining a deeper appreciation for its timeless wisdom.

Furthermore, the purpose of this book extends beyond mere intellectual inquiry to encompass the spiritual growth and edification of believers. Through the process of grappling with apparent contradictions, readers are invited to deepen their faith, cultivate a greater reverence for Scripture, and grow in their relationship with God. As Ephesians 4:15 encourages, believers are called to "speak the truth in love, growing in every way more and more like Christ."

All in all, the purpose and scope of this book is rooted in a passionate pursuit of truth and a desire to empower believers to engage with Scripture in a meaningful and transformative way. By addressing alleged contradictions with diligence and integrity, the book seeks to uphold the authority of God's Word and inspire a deeper commitment to its study and application in the lives of believers.

Importance of Addressing Alleged Contradictions:

Addressing alleged contradictions in the Bible holds significant importance for believers and skeptics alike. These apparent discrepancies, when left unexamined, can undermine the credibility and trustworthiness of Scripture. However, a closer examination often reveals that what initially appears contradictory may actually be reconcilable through careful study and interpretation.

Scripture itself encourages believers to diligently search for truth and understanding. In 2 Timothy 2:15, Paul instructs Timothy to "do your best to present yourself to God as one approved, a worker who has no need to be ashamed, rightly handling the word of truth." This underscores the importance of accurately interpreting and understanding Scripture. Additionally, 1 Peter 3:15 urges believers to "always be prepared to give an answer to everyone who asks you to give the reason for the hope that you have." Addressing alleged contradictions equips believers to engage in meaningful dialogue and defend their faith with confidence.

Moreover, addressing alleged contradictions fosters a deeper appreciation and understanding of the complexity and richness of Scripture. As Proverbs 25:2 states, "It is the glory of God to conceal things, but the glory of kings is to search things out." Engaging with apparent contradictions challenges believers to wrestle with the text, leading to spiritual growth and maturity.

Furthermore, addressing alleged contradictions helps to remove stumbling blocks for skeptics and seekers. When skeptics raise objections based on perceived contradictions, providing thoughtful and well-reasoned responses can lead to fruitful conversations and opportunities for evangelism. As 1 Corinthians 9:22 suggests, believers should be willing to "become all things to all people so that by all possible means I might save some."

Addressing alleged contradictions in the Bible is vital for upholding the integrity of Scripture, fostering a deeper understanding of God's Word, and effectively engaging with skeptics and seekers. It reflects a commitment to truth-seeking and strengthens the faith of believers while providing compelling reasons for others to consider the claims of Christianity.

Approach to Analyzing Contradictions:

The approach taken in this book towards analyzing alleged contradictions in the Bible is characterized by thoroughness, integrity, and a commitment to scholarly inquiry. Rather than dismissing apparent contradictions outright or offering simplistic explanations, each contradiction is subjected to careful scrutiny and rigorous examination.

The first step in this approach involves establishing a solid foundation of biblical hermeneutics and interpretation principles. By adhering to sound exegetical methods and respecting the original context, language, and cultural background of the biblical texts, readers are guided towards a deeper understanding of the passages in question.

Furthermore, this approach emphasizes the importance of engaging with diverse perspectives and interpretations. Recognizing that the Bible is a complex and multifaceted collection of writings spanning different genres, historical periods, and cultural contexts, readers are encouraged to consider a variety of viewpoints in their analysis.

Moreover, this approach seeks to integrate insights from biblical scholarship, theology, and apologetics into the analysis of alleged contradictions. By drawing on the expertise and research of scholars and theologians, readers gain access to valuable resources and perspectives that enrich their understanding of the text.

Central to this approach is the recognition that addressing alleged contradictions requires humility, open-mindedness, and a willingness to wrestle with difficult questions. Rather than seeking to impose preconceived notions or doctrinal frameworks onto the text, readers are invited into a process of discovery that values intellectual honesty and integrity.

Ultimately, the goal of this approach is not to provide definitive answers to every alleged contradiction but to foster a deeper appreciation for the complexity and depth of Scripture. By engaging in thoughtful dialogue and reflection, readers are empowered to navigate the tensions and challenges inherent in the biblical text with confidence and clarity.

Overview of the Outline:

The outline of this book is carefully structured to guide readers through a systematic examination of alleged contradictions in the Bible, offering a comprehensive framework for analysis and reflection. Each section of the outline is thoughtfully crafted to provide clarity and coherence, ensuring a cohesive and engaging reading experience.

The outline begins with an introduction that sets the stage for the exploration ahead, outlining the purpose and scope of the book, highlighting the importance of addressing alleged contradictions, and introducing the approach to analyzing these challenges.

Following the introduction, the outline unfolds into a series of chapters, each focusing on a specific alleged contradiction in the Bible. Each chapter is meticulously researched and presented in a consistent format, beginning with an introduction to the contradiction, followed by an analysis of the context, language, and historical background of the passage in question.

Moreover, each chapter offers a variety of interpretations and perspectives, drawing on insights from biblical scholarship, theology, and apologetics to provide readers with a comprehensive understanding of the issues at hand. The chapters conclude with a summary of findings and reflections on the significance of understanding the apparent contradiction.

In addition to addressing alleged contradictions, the outline includes sections devoted to broader themes and insights gleaned from the examination of these challenges. These sections provide readers with opportunities for deeper reflection and engagement, encouraging them to wrestle with the complexities of Scripture and grow in their faith. To study this book you need to have your bible with you at all times reading the scripture references first before turning to the book for deeper insights.

Chapter 2: Does The Bible Ever Contradict Itself?

- Contextual Analysis
- Theological Perspectives
- Faith and Interpretation
- Logical and Harmonization Approaches

This chapter delves into the intriguing question of whether the Bible contains contradictions. Through a multifaceted examination, we explore various aspects of this complex issue, aiming to shed light on the matter and provide clarity for readers.

1. Contextual Analysis:

We begin by emphasizing the crucial role of context in biblical interpretation. Understanding the historical, cultural, and linguistic context is essential for grasping the intended meaning of passages and discerning potential contradictions.

2. Theological Perspectives:

Next, we delve into the diverse approaches taken by different theological traditions when encountering alleged contradictions in the Bible. By exploring various theological frameworks, readers gain insight into how different perspectives shape interpretations of Scripture.

3. Faith and Interpretation:

This section delves into the intersection of faith and interpretation. We highlight the significance of faith in approaching the Bible and trusting in God's Word despite encountering perceived contradictions. Emphasizing the importance of maintaining trust and confidence in Scripture, we encourage readers to engage in interpretation with a faithful mindset.

4. Logical and Harmonization Approaches:

Lastly, we explore logical reasoning and harmonization methods employed in resolving alleged contradictions. By examining examples of harmonization techniques used by scholars and theologians, readers gain insight into how apparent contradictions can be reconciled through logical analysis and harmonization strategies.

1. Contextual Analysis:

Context plays a pivotal role in accurately interpreting the Bible. Without considering the context surrounding a passage, it's easy to misinterpret its meaning and potentially perceive contradictions where none exist. Context encompasses various elements, including historical, cultural, linguistic, and literary factors, all of which contribute to the richness and depth of biblical understanding.

Historical Context:

Examining the historical context involves understanding the social, political, and religious circumstances in which biblical texts were written. For example, understanding the political climate of ancient Israel during the time of the prophets provides insights into the messages they conveyed to their contemporaries. Historical context helps readers grasp the intended meaning of passages and avoid misinterpretations arising from anachronistic assumptions.

Another view may be considered in the prophecy of Isaiah concerning the fall of Babylon (Isaiah 13-14). Without historical context, readers may interpret this prophecy as a literal description of Babylon's destruction. However, historical records reveal that the fall of Babylon occurred at the hands of the Persians, not the Medes as Isaiah prophesied. Understanding the historical context helps reconcile apparent discrepancies between biblical prophecy and historical events.

Cultural Context:

Cultural context involves understanding the customs, traditions, beliefs, and societal norms prevalent during the time the biblical texts were composed. Biblical narratives often reflect the cultural milieu of ancient Near Eastern societies, including their agricultural practices, familial structures, and religious rituals. For instance, Jesus' parables often drew upon familiar cultural practices and imagery to convey spiritual truths.

In the Parable of the Good Samaritan (Luke 10:25-37), understanding the cultural animosity between Jews and Samaritans provides insights into the radical message of love and compassion conveyed by Jesus. Similarly, the cultural significance of hospitality in the ancient Near East enhances our understanding of the parable's message. By understanding the cultural context, readers can better appreciate the nuances of biblical teachings and avoid imposing modern cultural biases onto the text.

Linguistic Context:

Linguistic context pertains to the language and literary conventions employed in biblical texts. The Bible was written in ancient languages such as Hebrew, Aramaic, and Greek, each with its unique linguistic features and idiomatic expressions. Consider the Hebrew word "ruach," which is translated as "spirit" or "breath" in English. In Genesis 1:2, the "Spirit of God" (ruach Elohim) hovers over the waters, conveying the creative presence of God.

However, in Psalm 51:11, the same word is used to describe the "spirit" (ruach) of a person. Understanding the original languages and literary genres enables readers to grasp the nuances of biblical texts and discern the intended meaning behind words and phrases. Linguistic context also involves considering the broader literary context of passages within the larger narrative framework of biblical books.

Impact of Context on Interpretation:

The impact of historical, cultural, and linguistic context on biblical interpretation cannot be overstated. Context provides the necessary framework for understanding the motivations behind biblical authors, the intended audience of their writings, and the socio-cultural backdrop against which their messages were conveyed. By contextualizing biblical passages within their historical, cultural, and linguistic settings, readers can discern the underlying themes, motifs, and theological insights embedded within the text.

Illustrative Examples:

To illustrate the importance of contextual analysis, consider the interpretation of Jesus' parables. Without understanding the agricultural practices and social dynamics of first-century Palestine, readers may overlook the profound cultural insights conveyed through these parables. Similarly, understanding the historical context of Israel's exodus from Egypt illuminates the theological significance of the Passover ritual and its enduring relevance for Jewish identity.

To further illustrate the importance of contextual analysis, consider the Sermon on the Mount (Matthew 5-7). Jesus' teachings in this sermon reflect the socio-religious context of first-century Judaism, addressing issues such as righteousness, mercy, and the kingdom of God. Without understanding the cultural and religious milieu of Jesus' audience, readers may misinterpret his teachings and overlook their profound implications for discipleship.

Contextual analysis is essential for accurate biblical interpretation. By delving into the historical, cultural, and linguistic context of biblical texts, readers can gain deeper insights into the meaning of Scripture and avoid misinterpretations that may arise from neglecting context.

2. Theological Perspectives:

Disclaimer: This is just a snippet of the views from different theological point of views and more extensive research could be found in each's encyclopedia or library of resources. Different theological traditions within Christianity approach alleged contradictions in the Bible through distinct lenses, reflecting their unique doctrinal emphases, interpretive methods, and theological presuppositions.

1. Fundamentalist Perspective:

Fundamentalist theologians typically adhere to a literalist interpretation of Scripture, viewing the Bible as inerrant and without contradiction. They may employ harmonization methods to reconcile apparent discrepancies, emphasizing the unity and coherence of Scripture. For example, fundamentalists may interpret the creation narratives in Genesis 1 and 2 as complementary rather than contradictory, highlighting different aspects of the divine creative work.

2. Liberal Perspective:

Liberal theologians approach alleged contradictions with a critical and historical lens, acknowledging the human authorship and cultural conditioning of biblical texts. They may view apparent contradictions as indicative of the diverse theological viewpoints and evolving understandings within the biblical canon. Rather than seeking harmonization, liberals may embrace the tensions and diversity present in Scripture, recognizing the dynamic nature of theological discourse.

3. Catholic Perspective:

Catholic theology emphasizes the authority of tradition alongside Scripture, viewing the Church as the authoritative interpreter of divine revelation. Catholic theologians may approach alleged contradictions by appealing to the teachings of the Magisterium and the interpretive tradition of the Church. They may also emphasize the importance of allegorical and typological interpretations, discerning deeper spiritual meanings beneath the surface of apparent contradictions.

4. Evangelical Perspective:

Evangelical theologians affirm the authority of Scripture as the inspired Word of God while recognizing the human agency involved in its transmission. They may approach alleged contradictions by employing a hermeneutic of trust, trusting in the overall reliability and coherence of Scripture despite apparent discrepancies. Evangelicals may emphasize the role of the Holy Spirit in illuminating Scripture and guiding believers in interpretation.

Exploring Theological Frameworks for Understanding Scripture:

Theological frameworks provide lenses through which theologians interpret and understand Scripture. These frameworks shape how theologians approach alleged contradictions and seek to reconcile them within a broader theological context.

1. Covenant Theology:

Covenant theology views Scripture through the lens of God's covenantal relationship with humanity, tracing the overarching narrative of redemption from Genesis to Revelation. Covenant theologians may interpret alleged contradictions within the framework of God's covenantal promises and fulfillment in Christ, emphasizing continuity and fulfillment rather than contradiction.

2. Dispensationalism:

Dispensational theology divides biblical history into distinct dispensations or epochs, each characterized by different divine arrangements and responsibilities. Dispensationalists may approach alleged contradictions by distinguishing between different dispensations and interpreting them within their respective contexts. They may emphasize the progressive revelation of God's plan throughout history, reconciling apparent contradictions within the broader framework of God's sovereign purposes.

3. Liberation Theology:

Liberation theology emphasizes the socio-political dimensions of Scripture, interpreting it through the lens of liberation and social justice. Liberation theologians may approach alleged contradictions by highlighting the prophetic critique of oppression and injustice within Scripture. They may emphasize the liberating message of the gospel for marginalized and oppressed communities, seeking to address social contradictions through the transformative power of God's Word.

Theological perspectives and frameworks shape how theologians approach alleged contradictions in the Bible. By exploring diverse theological traditions and interpretive methods, readers gain insight into the multifaceted nature of biblical interpretation and the theological richness of Scripture

3. Faith and Interpretation:

Understanding the Role of Faith in Biblical Interpretation:

Faith serves as the cornerstone of biblical interpretation, shaping the way believers approach, engage with, and derive meaning from Scripture. At its core, faith involves a deep-seated trust in the divine origin, authority, and reliability of the Bible as the inspired Word of God. This trust extends beyond mere intellectual assent to encompass a profound conviction that Scripture carries transformative power and divine truth.

1. **Trust in God's Revelation**:

Central to faith-based biblical interpretation is the foundational belief in the divine inspiration of Scripture. Faith affirms that the Bible is not merely a human composition but a sacred text divinely inspired by God Himself. This conviction underpins the interpretive process, infusing it with a sense of reverence, humility, and spiritual discernment.

Faith acknowledges Scripture as the primary means through which God communicates His will, character, and redemptive purposes to humanity. Believers approach the Bible with the understanding that it serves as a conduit for encountering God's presence, hearing His voice, and receiving His guidance in all aspects of life.

2. **Personal Relationship with God:**

Faith fosters a dynamic, personal relationship between believers and God, which significantly influences their interpretation of Scripture. Through faith, individuals come to see the Bible not merely as a historical artifact or literary text but as a living and active word that speaks directly to their hearts and circumstances.

This relational aspect of faith imbues the interpretive process with intimacy, inviting believers to engage with Scripture as a means of encountering God Himself. Through prayer, meditation, and the indwelling presence of the Holy Spirit, believers cultivate a deep sense of communion with God as they delve into the pages of Scripture.

Emphasizing the Importance of Trusting God's Word Despite Perceived Contradictions:

Despite encountering apparent contradictions or tensions within Scripture, faith calls believers to maintain unwavering trust in the reliability and coherence of God's Word. Rather than viewing perceived contradictions as obstacles to faith, believers are challenged to approach them with confidence in God's faithfulness and wisdom.

1. Recognizing the Limitations of Human Understanding:

Faith humbly acknowledges the finite nature of human understanding and the inherent complexities of divine revelation. While some passages of Scripture may appear contradictory or challenging to reconcile, faith prompts believers to trust in God's overarching plan and purpose.

Believers recognize that their comprehension of Scripture is partial and imperfect, and they approach the interpretive task with humility, acknowledging their dependence on God's wisdom and guidance. Rather than seeking to resolve every perceived tension through human reasoning alone, faith encourages believers to submit to the sovereignty of God and trust in His ultimate control over all matters of interpretation.

2. Seeking Spiritual Discernment:

Faith empowers believers to seek spiritual discernment when navigating perceived contradictions or difficulties in Scripture. Through prayerful reflection, meditation on God's Word, and reliance on the illumination of the Holy Spirit, believers can gain insights into the deeper spiritual truths embedded within apparent tensions or paradoxes.

Faith encourages believers to approach Scripture with an open heart and mind, allowing the Holy Spirit to guide them into all truth. By seeking spiritual discernment, believers can transcend mere intellectual analysis and apprehend the deeper mysteries and insights that lie beneath the surface of Scripture.

3. Maintaining Confidence in God's Faithfulness:

Ultimately, faith calls believers to maintain unwavering confidence in the faithfulness and trustworthiness of God Himself. Despite the challenges posed by perceived contradictions or difficult passages, believers anchor their faith in the character of God, who is consistent, unchanging, and faithful to His promises.

Believers derive assurance from the overarching narrative of Scripture, which testifies to God's redemptive plan and His steadfast love for humanity. Trusting in God's faithfulness enables believers to navigate apparent contradictions with confidence, knowing that His truth transcends human understanding and His purposes will ultimately prevail.

Ultimately faith serves as the lens through which believers approach biblical interpretation, guiding them to trust in God's Word despite perceived contradictions. Through a deep-seated trust in the divine origin and authority of Scripture, a personal relationship with God, and a commitment to spiritual discernment, believers can engage with Scripture with humility, reverence, and confidence, allowing God to speak to them through His inspired Word.

4. Logical and Harmonization Approaches:

Exploring Logical Reasoning and Harmonization Methods in Resolving Alleged Contradictions:

The logical and harmonization approaches to resolving alleged contradictions in the Bible are vital components of biblical interpretation, requiring meticulous examination, analysis, and synthesis of biblical texts. These methods employ logical reasoning, contextual analysis, and harmonization techniques to demonstrate the compatibility and coherence of Scripture, addressing perceived discrepancies and enhancing understanding.

1. Logical Reasoning in Biblical Interpretation:

Logical reasoning plays a crucial role in assessing and resolving alleged contradictions in the Bible. It involves applying deductive and inductive reasoning to evaluate the logical coherence of biblical passages, identifying potential inconsistencies, and discerning patterns of reasoning within the text.

For example, consider the alleged contradiction between Matthew 27:5 and Acts 1:18 regarding the fate of Judas Iscariot. Matthew states that Judas hanged himself, while Acts describes his death as falling headlong and his body bursting open. Logical reasoning helps reconcile these accounts by considering the possibility that Judas initially hanged himself, and later, due to decomposition or intervention, his body fell and burst open, thus aligning both narratives.

2. Harmonization Methods:

Harmonization methods aim to reconcile apparent contradictions by integrating diverse biblical texts into a cohesive and consistent narrative. These methods involve contextual, literary, theological, and hermeneutical approaches to harmonizing Scripture, elucidating its meaning and resolving potential discrepancies.

a. Contextual Harmonization:

Contextual harmonization examines the broader historical, cultural, and linguistic contexts of biblical passages to reconcile apparent contradictions. For instance, understanding the cultural practices of ancient Israelites sheds light on seemingly conflicting accounts of events or customs.

b. <u>Literary Harmonization:</u>

Literary harmonization focuses on the literary structure and genre of biblical texts to reconcile apparent contradictions. Scholars analyze narrative techniques, rhetorical devices, and thematic motifs to discern patterns of continuity and coherence within the biblical narrative, ensuring harmonious interpretations.

c. <u>Theological Harmonization:</u>

Theological harmonization emphasizes theological themes and overarching principles that unify diverse biblical passages. By identifying theological motifs such as God's sovereignty, human sinfulness, and divine redemption, theologians highlight the underlying theological unity of Scripture, resolving apparent contradictions in light of theological truths.

d. <u>Harmonization through Progressive Revelation:</u>

Harmonization through progressive revelation acknowledges the dynamic nature of divine revelation throughout Scripture. This approach recognizes that God progressively reveals His truth over time, accommodating human limitations and cultural contexts while maintaining His overarching purposes, thereby harmonizing seemingly divergent passages.

e. <u>Hermeneutical Harmonization:</u>

Hermeneutical harmonization employs sound principles of biblical interpretation to reconcile apparent contradictions. By applying methods such as the analogy of faith, the analogy of Scripture, and the principle of progressive revelation, scholars seek to harmonize diverse biblical texts within a coherent interpretive framework, ensuring consistency and coherence.

Logical and harmonization approaches to resolving alleged contradictions in the Bible entail rigorous analysis and synthesis of biblical texts. By employing contextual, literary, theological, and hermeneutical methods, scholars and theologians elucidate the meaning of Scripture, affirming its reliability and authority as the inspired Word of God.

Examples of Harmonization Techniques Used by Scholars and Theologians:

Harmonization techniques employed by scholars and theologians play a crucial role in reconciling apparent contradictions within the Bible, ensuring a coherent and consistent interpretation of Scripture. These techniques involve a multifaceted approach that incorporates historical, literary, theological, and textual analyses. Here are further elaborations and examples of harmonization techniques used by scholars and theologians:

1. Composite Narratives:

One common harmonization technique involves recognizing that biblical narratives often provide complementary perspectives on events rather than contradictory accounts. For instance, the four Gospels present varying details of Jesus' life, teachings, and miracles. By synthesizing these accounts, scholars can create composite narratives that harmonize the details while preserving the unique theological emphases of each Gospel writer.

For example, the Gospel accounts of Jesus' crucifixion and resurrection may appear to have discrepancies in the sequence of events and the identities of the women who visited the tomb. However, by carefully comparing and harmonizing the Gospel narratives, scholars can construct a cohesive timeline that integrates all the details provided by the different Gospel writers.

2. Cultural Contextualization:

Understanding the cultural context of biblical texts is essential for harmonization. The ancient Near Eastern cultural milieu in which the Bible was written significantly influences its language, customs, and worldview. For instance, biblical narratives may contain idiomatic expressions, cultural practices, and symbolic imagery that require contextualization to interpret accurately.

By studying the historical and cultural background of biblical passages, scholars can uncover the underlying meaning behind apparent contradictions. For example, the Old Testament laws regarding cleanliness and purity may seem obsolete or contradictory from a modern perspective. However, understanding their cultural significance within the ancient Israelite society helps reconcile these laws with broader theological principles.

3. Theological Frameworks:

Theological frameworks provide overarching principles that guide interpretation and harmonization. These frameworks help scholars navigate complex theological issues and reconcile apparent contradictions within

Scripture. For example, the doctrine of biblical inspiration affirms that Scripture is divinely inspired and authoritative for faith and practice.

Within a theological framework, scholars approach apparent contradictions with the understanding that God's Word is inherently trustworthy and consistent. This theological perspective informs their interpretation and harmonization efforts, ensuring that the unity and coherence of Scripture are maintained.

4. Harmonization through Genre Analysis:

Different genres of literature in the Bible require distinct interpretive approaches. Scholars employ genre analysis to discern the literary conventions, purposes, and themes of biblical texts. For instance, the Gospels contain historical narratives, parables, discourses, and apocalyptic visions, each with its unique characteristics and interpretive challenges.

By identifying the genre of a biblical passage and understanding its literary context, scholars can harmonize apparent contradictions by interpreting the text according to its intended genre. For example, interpreting a parable as an allegorical story meant to convey spiritual truths requires a different approach than interpreting a historical narrative describing factual events.

5. Textual Criticism:

Textual criticism involves the comparison of various manuscript traditions to determine the most accurate reading of the biblical text. Apparent contradictions may arise from textual variants or scribal errors introduced during the transmission of the biblical manuscripts. Scholars apply textual criticism principles to identify and resolve discrepancies, ensuring the reliability and accuracy of the biblical text.

For example, textual variants in the New Testament manuscripts may affect the wording or order of certain passages, leading to perceived contradictions in different manuscript traditions. By carefully evaluating the manuscript evidence and applying textual criticism methods, scholars can reconstruct the original text of Scripture and resolve apparent contradictions.

6. Harmonization by Progressive Revelation:

The principle of progressive revelation recognizes that God's revelation unfolds progressively throughout Scripture. As God's plan of redemption unfolds over time, later biblical texts may provide additional insights that clarify or expand upon earlier revelations. Scholars trace the development of theological themes and concepts throughout Scripture, harmonizing apparent contradictions by considering the broader scope of divine revelation.

For instance, the concept of salvation by grace through faith is progressively revealed in both the Old and New Testaments. While the Old Testament emphasizes God's covenant with Israel and the importance of obedience to the Law, the New Testament further develops the theme of salvation through the sacrificial death and resurrection of Jesus Christ. By tracing this theme of salvation through Scripture, scholars harmonize apparent contradictions and demonstrate the unity of God's redemptive plan.

Chapter 3: Understanding Alleged Contradictions

- Defining Contradictions
- Common Types of Alleged Contradictions
- Reasons for Alleged Contradictions

This chapter serves as a foundational exploration into the nature of alleged contradictions in the Bible. Readers are introduced to the concept of contradictions and guided through a comprehensive understanding of their various forms and manifestations within Scripture.

By delving into the definitions, common types, and underlying reasons for alleged contradictions, readers are equipped with essential knowledge and insights to navigate the complexities of biblical interpretation.

Through this exploration, readers are prepared for the in-depth analysis and examination of specific contradictions that will follow in subsequent chapters, fostering a deeper understanding and appreciation for the nuances of Scripture.

Defining Contradictions:

The concept of contradictions within the Bible is a topic that has intrigued scholars and theologians for centuries. At its core, a contradiction can be understood as a statement or proposition that directly conflicts with another statement or proposition, resulting in logical inconsistency or incompatibility. However, when it comes to defining contradictions within the context of Scripture, the issue becomes more complex due to the multifaceted nature of the biblical text.

One common approach to defining contradictions in the Bible is to consider them in terms of factual discrepancies or inconsistencies between different passages or accounts. For example, some alleged contradictions may arise from variations in details between parallel passages in the Gospels, such as differences in the timing or sequence of events surrounding Jesus' ministry.

Scripture itself acknowledges the importance of accuracy and consistency in conveying truth. Proverbs 30:5 declares, "Every word of God proves true; he is a shield to those who take refuge in him." This emphasizes the foundational belief among believers in the reliability and trustworthiness of God's Word.

However, it is essential to recognize that not all apparent discrepancies in Scripture necessarily constitute contradictions in the strictest sense. Some alleged contradictions may stem from differences in literary genres, cultural contexts, or theological perspectives, which require careful consideration and interpretation.

Moreover, biblical scholars and theologians often approach the issue of contradictions with nuance and sophistication, recognizing the need to interpret Scripture within its broader context and theological framework. For example, differences in genealogies between different books of the Bible may reflect theological emphases rather than factual discrepancies.

Furthermore, historical and archaeological research can shed light on apparent contradictions by providing insights into the cultural and historical contexts in which the biblical texts were written. By understanding the social customs, linguistic conventions, and literary techniques of ancient Near Eastern cultures, scholars can gain a deeper appreciation for the complexities of biblical interpretation.

Common Types of Alleged Contradictions:

Alleged contradictions within the Bible manifest in various forms, reflecting the diverse nature of the biblical text and the complexities of interpretation. While some contradictions may appear straightforward, others require nuanced analysis and consideration of contextual factors. Understanding the common types of alleged contradictions provides a framework for identifying and addressing these challenges effectively.

1. Chronological Discrepancies:

One common type of alleged contradiction involves differences in the timing or sequence of events presented in different passages of Scripture. For example, discrepancies in the order of events surrounding Jesus' crucifixion and resurrection in the Gospels have been the subject of scholarly debate. However, such variations may be attributed to differences in the authors' literary purposes or perspectives rather than factual contradictions.

2. Geographical Discrepancies:

Another type of alleged contradiction pertains to differences in geographical details presented in different biblical accounts. These variations may include differences in place names, distances, or geographical features. For instance, variations in the details of Paul's conversion experience as recounted in Acts 9, 22, and 26 have been cited as potential contradictions. However, such differences may be attributed to variations in oral tradition, editorial decisions, or the author's theological emphases.

3. Theological Discrepancies:

Alleged contradictions may also arise from differences in theological teachings or perspectives presented in different passages of Scripture. These variations may include differences in doctrinal emphases, theological interpretations, or ethical teachings. For example, variations in the details of salvation and justification presented in the Pauline epistles and the book of James have been the subject of theological debate. However, such differences may reflect complementary rather than contradictory perspectives on faith and works.

4. Numerical Discrepancies:

Alleged contradictions may involve differences in numerical details presented in different biblical accounts. These variations may include differences in numbers, measurements, or quantities mentioned in various passages. For example, variations in the number of soldiers reported in the accounts of David's census in 2 Samuel 24 and 1 Chronicles 21 have been cited as potential contradictions. However, such differences may be attributed to textual variants, editorial decisions, or different counting methods.

5. Textual Discrepancies:

Alleged contradictions may also arise from differences in textual details presented in different manuscript traditions or versions of the Bible. These variations may include differences in wording, syntax, or punctuation found in different copies of the biblical text. For example, variations in the wording of the Lord's Prayer as recorded in Matthew 6:9-13 and Luke 11:2-4 have been the subject of textual criticism. However, such differences may reflect variations in oral tradition, translation practices, or scribal errors rather than factual contradictions.

Understanding the common types of alleged contradictions within the Bible is essential for effectively addressing these challenges and navigating the complexities of biblical interpretation. By recognizing the diverse forms in which alleged contradictions may arise, readers can approach the study of Scripture with discernment, humility, and a commitment to seeking truth. Through careful analysis and interpretation, believers can deepen their understanding of God's Word and enrich their faith journey.

Reasons for Alleged Contradictions:

The presence of alleged contradictions within the Bible has been a subject of debate and inquiry among scholars, theologians, and believers for centuries. While these contradictions may appear to challenge the integrity and reliability of Scripture, a closer examination reveals several underlying reasons and contributing factors that help to contextualize and understand their occurrence.

1. Human Authorship and Perspectives:

One reason for alleged contradictions in the Bible is the diverse human authorship and perspectives represented within its pages. The Bible is composed of various books written by multiple authors over centuries, each with their own unique backgrounds, experiences, and literary styles. As a result, differences in emphasis, language, and narrative style may give rise to apparent contradictions. For example, variations in the details of Jesus' genealogy presented in Matthew 1 and Luke 3 may reflect the authors' theological and literary purposes rather than factual discrepancies.

2. Oral Tradition and Transmission:

Another reason for alleged contradictions relates to the oral tradition and transmission of biblical texts over time. Before the advent of writing, the stories, teachings, and accounts contained within the Bible were passed down orally through generations. As a result, variations and discrepancies may have arisen in the retelling and transmission of these narratives. For example, variations in the details of Jesus' resurrection appearances as recounted in the Gospels may be attributed to differences in oral traditions and eyewitness testimonies.

3. Literary and Theological Emphases:

Alleged contradictions may also arise from differences in the literary and theological emphases of biblical authors. Each author of the Bible wrote with specific purposes and audiences in mind, shaping their narratives and teachings accordingly. These differences in emphasis may lead to variations in details and perspectives, which may be perceived as contradictions. For example, differences in the accounts of Jesus' temptation in the wilderness as presented in Matthew 4 and Luke 4 may reflect the authors' theological emphases and narrative structures.

4. Textual Transmission and Variants:

Variations in the textual transmission of biblical manuscripts and the presence of textual variants may contribute to alleged contradictions. Over time, copyists and scribes hand-copied biblical manuscripts, leading to differences in wording, spelling, and punctuation. While the majority of textual variants are minor and do not affect the overall meaning of the text, some may give rise to apparent contradictions. For example, variations in the wording of Jesus' final words on the cross as recorded in Matthew 27:46 and Mark 15:34 may be attributed to textual variants.

5. Cultural and Historical Context:

The cultural and historical context in which biblical texts were written may also play a role in the occurrence of alleged contradictions. The Bible was written in ancient times and within specific cultural and historical contexts that may be unfamiliar to modern readers. As a result, differences in cultural practices, linguistic conventions, and historical perspectives may contribute to apparent contradictions. For example, variations in the details of Paul's conversion experience as recounted in Acts 9, 22, and 26 may reflect differences in historical accounts and cultural contexts.

The reasons for alleged contradictions within the Bible requires careful consideration of the diverse factors at play, including human authorship, oral tradition, literary and theological emphases, textual transmission, and cultural context. By recognizing these underlying factors, readers can approach alleged contradictions with humility, discernment, and a commitment to seeking truth, enriching their understanding of Scripture and deepening their faith journey.

Chapter 4: Examining Alleged Contradictions

31

1. Order of Creation

Scripture References:

Genesis 1:1-31

Genesis 2:4-25

<u>Analysis</u>

The supposed contradiction in Genesis lies in the order of creation between two passages:

•Genesis 1:

This chapter presents a broader creation story, describing the creation of the world in six days. It follows a sequence where:

1. Light is separated from darkness (Day 1)

2. The firmament (sky) is separated from the waters (Day 2)

3. Land is separated from the water and dry land appears (Day 3)

4. The sun, moon, and stars are created (Day 4)

5. Creatures of the sea and air are created (Day 5)

6. Land animals and humans are created (Day 6)

•Genesis 2:

This chapter offers a more detailed account of God creating humanity and the Garden of Eden. Here, the creation seems to happen in a slightly different order:

1. Man is formed from the dust of the ground (v. 7)

2. The garden is planted by God (v. 8-9)

3. The animals are formed from the ground (v. 19)

4. Woman is created from man's rib (v. 21-22)

The main point of contention is the creation of plants and animals. Genesis 1 suggests they were created before humans (Day 3 for plants and Day 5 for animals), while Genesis 2 seems to imply they were created after (v. 19 for animals).

Context:

Genesis 1 presents a structured and systematic account of creation, divided into six days. Each day brings forth new elements of creation, culminating in the creation of humanity on the sixth day. In contrast, Genesis 2 zooms in on the creation of humanity, providing a more detailed narrative that focuses specifically on the formation of Adam and the establishment of the Garden of Eden.

Language:

The Hebrew language used in Genesis 1 and Genesis 2 provides insights into the creative acts of God. In Genesis 1, the word "create" (bara) emphasizes the divine act of bringing something into existence out of nothing. This term underscores God's sovereign power as the Creator of all things.

On the other hand, Genesis 2 uses the word "formed" (yatsar), which implies shaping or molding something that already exists. This term highlights the intimate and hands-on involvement of God in the creation of humanity, suggesting a more personal and relational aspect to the creative process.

Historical Background:

To understand the creation narratives in Genesis, it's essential to consider the historical and cultural context of the ancient Near East. These accounts were written within a specific cultural milieu, shaped by the religious beliefs and cosmology of the ancient Israelites. The creation narratives in Genesis reflect the broader ancient Near Eastern worldview, presenting God as the supreme Creator who brings order out of chaos.

Theological Considerations:

Both Genesis 1 and Genesis 2 convey profound theological truths about God's character and His relationship with humanity. These narratives emphasize God's sovereignty, creativity, and care for His creation. Additionally, they highlight the unique role of humanity as made in the image of God and entrusted with stewardship over the earth.

Insights from Scholars, Theologians, and Apologists:

<u>Various Interpretations and Perspectives:</u>

1. Literal vs. Literary Interpretation: Some scholars and theologians propose that the apparent differences in the creation order between Genesis 1 and Genesis 2 are due to the different literary styles and theological emphases of each chapter. While Genesis 1 presents a structured, sequential account of creation, Genesis 2 offers a more focused narrative that zooms in on the creation of humanity. These scholars argue that attempting to harmonize the

two accounts by aligning them chronologically may overlook the theological richness and literary nuances of the texts.

2. Complementary Accounts: Other scholars suggest that Genesis 1 and Genesis 2 present complementary rather than contradictory accounts of creation. They argue that Genesis 1 provides a broad overview of the entire creation week, emphasizing the grandeur and majesty of God's creative acts, while Genesis 2 offers a more detailed focus on the creation of humanity and the establishment of the Garden of Eden. From this perspective, the two chapters supplement each other, providing different perspectives on the same event rather than presenting conflicting narratives.

3. Literary Structure and Theological Themes: Some scholars emphasize the distinct literary structures and theological themes present in Genesis 1 and Genesis 2. Genesis 1 follows a structured pattern of "days" or "epochs," highlighting God's orderly and purposeful creation of the cosmos. In contrast, Genesis 2 employs a more narrative style, focusing on the intimate relationship between God and humanity and the special role assigned to humanity as stewards of creation. While the two chapters may differ in their presentation, they share common theological themes such as the goodness of creation, the sovereignty of God, and the unique dignity of humanity.

4. Cultural and Historical Context: Scholars also consider the cultural and historical context in which Genesis was written. Ancient Near Eastern creation accounts often employed symbolic language and theological motifs to convey deeper truths about the nature of the universe and humanity's place within it. In this light, the differences between Genesis 1 and Genesis 2 may reflect the author's use of familiar literary conventions to communicate profound theological truths rather than providing a scientific or historical chronology of events.

Summary and Reflection:

Despite the apparent differences in the creation order between Genesis 1 and Genesis 2, these passages affirm the theological unity and coherence of the biblical creation accounts. Understanding the literary genres, cultural contexts, and theological themes of these passages is crucial for interpreting them faithfully. Ultimately, both narratives convey profound truths about God's creative power, His relationship with humanity, and the purpose of creation and no contradiction whatsoever.

2. Number of Animals on Noah's Ark

Scripture References:

Genesis 6:19-20

Genesis 7:2-3

<u>Analysis</u>

The supposed contradiction in the number of animals on Noah's Ark comes from two passages in Genesis:

Genesis 6:19:

"And of every living thing of all flesh, you shall bring two of every sort into the ark, to keep them alive with you. They shall be male and female." (NIV)

This verse seems to indicate that Noah brought two of each animal onto the ark.

Genesis 7:2-3:

"You shall take with you seven each of every kind of clean animal, a male and its female, and two each of every kind of unclean animal, a male and its female, also seven each of the birds of the heavens, male and female, to keep their offspring alive on the face of all the earth." (NIV)

Here, the passage specifies seven of each clean animal and two of each unclean animal. This difference creates a question: Did Noah take two of each animal or seven of each clean animal?

Context:

Genesis 6:19-20 records God's initial instructions to Noah regarding the animals to be taken on the ark: "You are to bring into the ark two of all living creatures, male and female, to keep them alive with you.

Two of every kind of bird, of every kind of animal and of every kind of creature that moves along the ground will come to you to be kept alive." This passage seems to indicate that Noah was instructed to bring only two of every kind of animal onto the ark.

However, Genesis 7:2-3 provides additional instructions to Noah: "Take with you seven pairs of every kind of clean animal, a male and its mate, and one pair of every kind of unclean animal, a male and its mate, and also seven pairs of every kind of bird, male and female, to keep their various kinds alive throughout the earth." Here, the instructions specify the inclusion of seven pairs of every clean animal and one pair of every unclean animal, along with seven pairs of every kind of bird.

Language:

The language used in Genesis emphasizes God's command to Noah to gather the animals for preservation during the flood. The terms "every living creature" and "every kind of animal" denote a broad range of species, suggesting a comprehensive collection of the animal kingdom to ensure their survival.

Historical Background:

The historical context of the flood narrative in Genesis reflects ancient Near Eastern cosmology and worldview. The account of the flood is portrayed as a global event in Genesis and regardless of the extent of the flood, the narrative presents the ark as a means of preserving animal life during the cataclysmic event.

Theological Considerations:

The flood narrative in Genesis emphasizes God's judgment on human wickedness and His provision for the preservation of life through Noah and the ark. The account underscores God's sovereignty over creation and His faithfulness to His covenant promises. The preservation of the animals on the ark demonstrates God's care for His creation and His desire to sustain life even in the midst of judgment.

Insights from Scholars, Theologians, and Apologists

<u>Various Interpretations and Perspectives:</u>

1. Literal vs. Figurative Interpretation: Some interpreters approach the account of Noah's Ark literally, understanding it as a historical event where Noah gathered pairs of every animal onto the ark. Others view the narrative more figuratively, seeing it as a symbolic representation of God's judgment on sin and His provision for salvation through faith.

2. Logistic Challenges: Critics of the account of Noah's Ark often raise logistical challenges regarding the feasibility of fitting all known animal species onto the ark. However, proponents of the biblical narrative argue that the focus of the account is not on cataloging every species but on highlighting God's preservation of life through Noah and the ark.

3. Representation vs. Exhaustive Collection: Some scholars suggest that the instruction to bring "two of every kind of living creature" may be understood in terms of representative pairs rather than an exhaustive collection of every

species. In this view, Noah would have gathered representatives of each kind of animal onto the ark, ensuring the survival of their respective species.

4. Divine Intervention: Others point to the possibility of divine intervention in the gathering of the animals, suggesting that God supernaturally guided the animals to the ark or temporarily suspended the laws of nature to facilitate their gathering. This perspective highlights the miraculous nature of the flood narrative and God's sovereignty over creation.

Summary and Reflection:

The account of Noah's Ark presents a challenging yet profound narrative that raises questions about the logistics and feasibility of gathering animals onto the ark. While skeptics may point to apparent contradictions regarding the number and diversity of animals, believers find assurance in the theological significance of the narrative—the sovereignty of God.

His judgment on sin, and His provision for salvation through faith. Ultimately, the flood narrative serves as a powerful reminder of God's faithfulness to His covenant promises and His care for His creation. There is no contradiction, only a deeper invitation to explore the depths of God's providence and grace.

3. Length of the Israelites' Sojourn in Egypt

Scripture References:

Genesis 15:13-14

Exodus 12:40-41

<u>Analysis</u>

The supposed contradiction lies in the length of time the Israelites spent in Egypt. Here's the breakdown:

Genesis 15:13

God tells Abraham his descendants "shall be sojourners in a land that is not theirs, and they will serve them and be afflicted by them four hundred years." (NIV)

Exodus 12:40

The Israelites' time in Egypt is described as lasting "four hundred thirty years." (NIV)

The difference is 430 years on one passage and 400 years on another passage which basically is 30 years. This is a common question among scholars who study the Bible, the explanations below will offer some possibilities for reconciling the apparent contradiction.

Context:

In Genesis 15:13-14, God speaks to Abram (later known as Abraham) and foretells the future affliction and liberation of his descendants. God informs Abram that his descendants will be strangers in a foreign land, where they will be enslaved and oppressed for 400 years. This prophecy sets the stage for the Israelites' eventual sojourn in Egypt and their deliverance by God.

In Exodus 12:40-41, the account of the Israelites' departure from Egypt provides a specific timeframe for their time in Egypt. It states that the length of time the Israelites lived in Egypt was 430 years to the very day. This timeframe encompasses the period from the arrival of Jacob and his family in Egypt to the exodus led by Moses.

Language:

In Genesis 15, the language used to describe the duration of the Israelites' affliction in a foreign land is symbolic and prophetic. The 400-year timeframe represents a period of oppression and hardship rather than an exact chronological duration. This symbolic language underscores the inevitability and severity of the Israelites' suffering before their eventual liberation.

In Exodus 12, the language used to describe the length of the Israelites' time in Egypt is more specific and precise. The text states that the Israelites lived in Egypt for 430 years, providing a clear timeframe for their sojourn in the land of their captivity.

Historical Background:

To understand the discrepancy between the timeframes mentioned in Genesis 15 and Exodus 12, it's essential to consider the historical context of the Israelites' sojourn in Egypt. The 400-year period mentioned in Genesis 15 likely includes the entire duration from the arrival of Jacob and his family in Egypt to the exodus. This period encompasses the patriarchal period, the enslavement of the Israelites, and their eventual deliverance.

The 430-year period mentioned in Exodus 12 specifically refers to the time the Israelites lived in Egypt, from the arrival of Jacob's family until their departure under the leadership of Moses. This timeframe aligns with the chronological account of events leading up to the exodus and emphasizes the fulfillment of God's promise to deliver His people.

Theological Considerations:

Both Genesis 15 and Exodus 12 convey important theological truths about God's faithfulness to His promises and His sovereignty over history. Genesis 15 emphasizes God's prophetic foresight and His commitment to fulfilling His covenant promises to Abraham and his descendants. Exodus 12 underscores God's decisive action in redeeming His people from bondage and establishing them as a nation.

Insights from Scholars, Theologians, and Apologists

<u>Various Interpretations and Perspectives:</u>

1. Symbolic Interpretation: Some scholars propose a symbolic interpretation of the numbers mentioned in Genesis 15 and Exodus 12. They suggest that the 400 years in Genesis 15 may represent a round number or a symbolic period rather than a precise timeframe. Similarly, the 430 years in Exodus 12 could symbolize the entire period of the Israelites' sojourn in Egypt, including both the time of affliction and the exodus. From this perspective, the discrepancy in the numbers does not necessarily indicate a contradiction but reflects the symbolic nature of biblical language and prophecy.

2. Historical Context: The historical context of the Israelites' sojourn in Egypt is crucial for understanding the timeframe mentioned in these passages. Scholars consider factors such as the arrival of Jacob and his family in Egypt, the oppression of the Israelites by the Egyptians, and their eventual liberation under Moses' leadership. By examining archaeological evidence, ancient texts, and cultural practices, theologians can reconstruct the historical timeline and discern the accuracy of the biblical narrative.

3. Theological Significance: The discrepancy between the numbers in Genesis 15 and Exodus 12 raises theological questions about the nature of biblical prophecy and inspiration. Some theologians emphasize the overarching theological themes conveyed in these passages, such as God's faithfulness to His promises, His sovereignty over history, and His deliverance of His people from bondage. While the precise timeframe may be debated, the theological significance of the Israelites' liberation remains central to the biblical narrative.

4. Harmonization Methods: Apologists offer various harmonization methods to reconcile the apparent contradiction between Genesis 15 and Exodus 12. These methods include considering the possibility of overlapping or complementary timeframes, accounting for different historical perspectives, and recognizing the symbolic or prophetic nature of the numbers mentioned in the text. By examining the broader context of the biblical narrative and interpreting the passages in light of their literary, cultural, and theological backgrounds, scholars can harmonize apparent discrepancies and discern the deeper truths conveyed in Scripture.

5. Faith and Interpretation: Ultimately, the interpretation of biblical passages involves faith in God's revelation and trust in His guidance. While scholars may offer different perspectives and interpretations, believers rely on the Holy Spirit to illuminate the meaning of Scripture and guide them in understanding its truths. By approaching the text with humility, prayer, and a willingness to engage with different viewpoints, Christians can deepen their understanding of God's Word and grow in their faith journey.

Summary and Reflection:

The apparent contradiction between the timeframes mentioned in Genesis 15 and Exodus 12 underscores the complexity of interpreting biblical prophecy and historical narrative. While the symbolic and prophetic language of Genesis

15 provides a broad prediction of the Israelites' future affliction and deliverance, the historical account presented in Exodus 12 offers a specific timeframe for their sojourn in Egypt.

By reconciling these perspectives and considering the broader theological themes of the biblical narrative, scholars, theologians, and apologists can discern the deeper truths conveyed in Scripture. Ultimately, the discrepancies between these passages do not detract from the overarching message of God's faithfulness to His promises and His sovereignty over history. Instead, they invite readers to engage with the text critically and discern its intended meaning within its original context.

4. The Ten Commandments

Scripture References:

Exodus 20:1-17

Deuteronomy 5:6-21

<u>Analysis</u>

The supposed contradiction in the Ten Commandments lies not in the core message, but in the specific wording and details between Exodus 20 (often referred to as the "E source") and Deuteronomy 5 (the "D source"). Here's a breakdown of the differences:

Numbering:

- In Exodus 20, the commandment prohibiting worshipping other gods comes first.
- In Deuteronomy 5, the commandment regarding honoring parents comes first.
- This difference might be due to the emphasis the author wanted to place on a specific commandment.

Wording:

- There are slight variations in wording between the two passages. For example, Exodus 20:5 mentions "visiting the iniquity of the fathers on the children," which is absent in Deuteronomy 5.

Additional Details:

- Deuteronomy 5 adds some explanatory details to certain commandments, such as reminding the Israelites of their deliverance from Egypt when discussing the Sabbath.

These differences are not necessarily contradictions in the core principles. However, they raise questions about the origin and transmission of the Ten Commandments.

Context:

In understanding the variations between Exodus 20 and Deuteronomy 5 regarding the presentation of the Ten Commandments, it's crucial to consider the broader historical and narrative context of these texts. Exodus 20 occurs within the narrative of Israel's exodus from Egypt and their subsequent journey to Mount Sinai.

At Mount Sinai, God establishes a covenant with the Israelites and delivers the law, including the Ten Commandments, as a foundational framework for their covenant relationship. The context of Exodus 20 emphasizes the immediate aftermath of Israel's deliverance from slavery and their encounter with God's holiness and sovereignty.

On the other hand, Deuteronomy 5 takes place several decades later on the plains of Moab, as the new generation of Israelites prepares to enter the Promised Land. Moses, now addressing the new generation, recounts the giving of the law and the covenant renewal ceremony at Mount Sinai. The context of Deuteronomy 5 emphasizes the importance of obedience to the law as the Israelites prepare to inherit the land promised to their ancestors.

Language:

The variations in language and phrasing between Exodus 20 and Deuteronomy 5 reflect the flexibility and adaptability of ancient Near Eastern languages and textual traditions. In Exodus 20, the language used to convey the commandments is direct and authoritative, reflecting the solemnity of the covenantal ceremony at Mount Sinai. The wording emphasizes God's absolute authority and the imperative nature of the commandments.

In contrast, Deuteronomy 5 employs a more rhetorical and exhortative style, as Moses addresses the new generation of Israelites. The language used in Deuteronomy 5 emphasizes the importance of obedience and faithfulness to the covenant, urging the people to heed God's commands as they prepare to enter the Promised Land.

Historical Background:

The variations between Exodus 20 and Deuteronomy 5 may also be influenced by differences in historical context and transmission. The events described in Exodus 20 occur shortly after the exodus from Egypt, during a time of national covenant renewal and covenant establishment. The commandments are given as part of the covenantal ceremony at Mount Sinai, marking the beginning of Israel's journey as a covenant community.

In contrast, the events described in Deuteronomy 5 take place decades later, as the new generation of Israelites stands on the brink of entering the Promised Land. Moses, now an elder statesman, recounts the giving of the law and the covenant renewal ceremony to the new generation, emphasizing the importance of obedience and fidelity to the covenant.

Theological Considerations:

From a theological perspective, the variations between Exodus 20 and Deuteronomy 5 underscore the dynamic nature of biblical revelation and interpretation. The Ten Commandments serve as a foundational framework for Israel's covenant relationship with God, providing moral guidance and principles for righteous living.

Despite differences in language and presentation, the core principles and moral imperatives of the commandments remain consistent across both versions. The theological significance of the commandments lies in their role as a reflection of God's character and will for His people.

They embody God's holiness, justice, and mercy, calling His people to a life of obedience, righteousness, and compassion. The variations between Exodus 20 and Deuteronomy 5 highlight the diverse literary styles, theological emphases, and historical contexts within the biblical text, enriching our understanding of God's word and its application to our lives.

Insights from Scholars, Theologians, and Apologists

<u>Various Interpretations and Perspectives:</u>

1. Literary Structure: Scholars note that while both Exodus 20 and Deuteronomy 5 contain the listing of the Ten Commandments, they present them in slightly different ways.

Exodus 20 records the giving of the commandments directly from God to the Israelites at Mount Sinai, while Deuteronomy 5 recounts Moses' reiteration of the commandments to the new generation of Israelites before they enter the Promised Land.

Despite these differences in context and presentation, the content of the commandments remains consistent between the two passages.

2. Historical Context: Understanding the historical context of the Israelites' journey from Egypt to the Promised Land sheds light on the purpose and significance of the repetition of the Ten Commandments in Deuteronomy.

As the Israelites prepare to enter the land of Canaan, Moses delivers a series of speeches summarizing the law and renewing the covenant between God and His people. Deuteronomy serves as a reminder of God's faithfulness and a call to obedience as the Israelites prepare to inherit the land promised to their ancestors.

3. Theological Themes: The repetition of the Ten Commandments in Deuteronomy emphasizes key theological themes such as covenant, obedience, and faithfulness. By reiterating the commandments to a new generation, Moses underscores the enduring significance of God's moral law for His people.

The commandments serve as a foundation for righteous living and a guide for the Israelites' relationship with God and one another. Despite the passage of time and changing circumstances, the principles embodied in the commandments remain timeless and relevant for God's people.

4. Interpretive Perspectives: Scholars offer various interpretive perspectives to reconcile the differences between Exodus 20 and Deuteronomy 5. Some propose that the variations in wording and phrasing reflect the adaptability of the commandments to different contexts and audiences.

Others suggest that the repetition of the commandments in Deuteronomy serves as a rhetorical device to emphasize their importance and ensure their transmission to future generations. By examining the broader literary and theological themes of the Pentateuch, scholars can discern the unity and coherence of the biblical narrative despite apparent discrepancies in wording.

5. Faith and Application: For believers, the repetition of the Ten Commandments in Deuteronomy serves as a reminder of the enduring moral standards established by God for His people. While the specific wording may vary between Exodus and Deuteronomy, the underlying principles of love for God and neighbor remain unchanged.

Christians affirm the continued relevance of the commandments in guiding their lives and shaping their ethical decisions. By studying the commandments in their original context and applying them to contemporary situations, believers seek to honor God and live faithfully according to His Word.

Summary and Reflection:

The apparent differences between the listings of the Ten Commandments in Exodus 20 and Deuteronomy 5 highlight the complexity of biblical interpretation and the richness of the biblical narrative. While scholars may debate the reasons for these variations, believers affirm the unity and coherence of Scripture as inspired by God.

The repetition of the commandments in Deuteronomy serves as a testimony to the enduring significance of God's moral law and His faithfulness to His covenant with His people. As Christians seek to live according to God's commandments, they find assurance in His steadfast love and guidance throughout history.

5. David's Census

Scripture References:
- 2 Samuel 24
- 1 Chronicles 21

<u>Analysis</u>

The supposed contradiction in David's census lies in the reported number of Israelites counted. Here's a breakdown:

2 Samuel 24:9:

States there were 800,000 valiant men of Israel and 500,000 men of Judah who could draw the sword.

1 Chronicles 21:5:

Reports 1,100,000 men of Israel and 470,000 men of Judah who drew the sword.

This difference in numbers is a major point of discussion for biblical scholars. This is a well-known discrepancy in the Bible. Scholars don't have a definitive answer, but the explanations below offer some possibilities for reconciling the difference.

Context:

The census undertaken by David, as chronicled in 2 Samuel 24 and 1 Chronicles 21, occurs during a pivotal period in Israel's history, towards the latter part of David's reign as king. David's decision to conduct a census reflects the political and military climate of the time, as he sought to assess the strength and resources of his kingdom.

However, the act of taking a census carried deeper implications beyond mere enumeration; it signified a shift towards reliance on human strength rather than trust in God's providence. This context sets the stage for understanding the significance and consequences of David's actions.

Language:

The language used in the accounts of David's census underscores the gravity of his decision and the subsequent repercussions for Israel. In 2 Samuel 24, David's motivation for the census is attributed to his pride and arrogance, leading to God's displeasure and judgment upon the nation.

Conversely, 1 Chronicles 21 presents a more subdued portrayal of David's actions, focusing on the broader implications for Israel rather than delving into David's personal motivations. The choice of language in each narrative shapes the reader's understanding of David's character and the divine response to his actions.

Historical Background:

The historical backdrop against which David's census takes place provides crucial context for interpreting the events. During David's reign, Israel experienced both internal stability and external threats, necessitating vigilant leadership and military preparedness.

David's decision to conduct a census may have been influenced by geopolitical concerns, as he sought to strengthen his kingdom against potential adversaries. However, the biblical accounts suggest that David's reliance on human strength and worldly wisdom instead of trusting in God's guidance led to dire consequences for himself and the nation.

Theological Considerations:

From a theological perspective, the apparent contradiction between 2 Samuel 24 and 1 Chronicles 21 raises profound questions about divine sovereignty, human agency, and the nature of sin. Both narratives underscore God's authority over human affairs and His righteous judgment upon disobedience.

However, they present differing perspectives on the origin and consequences of David's actions. In 2 Samuel 24, God's wrath is directed towards David for his sinful pride, resulting in a devastating plague upon Israel.

In contrast, 1 Chronicles 21 portrays Satan as the instigator of the census, with God allowing the resulting judgment as a form of discipline. These theological nuances invite reflection on the complexities of divine justice and the intricacies of God's interaction with His creation.

Insights from Scholars, Theologians, and Apologists

<u>Various Interpretations and Perspectives:</u>

1. Literary Parallels: Some scholars interpret the variations between 2 Samuel 24 and 1 Chronicles 21 as literary parallels rather than contradictions. They suggest that the differences in language, perspective, and theological emphasis serve to enrich the narrative and provide complementary insights into David's reign and the consequences of his actions.

2. Theological Reflections: Others view the variations between the two accounts as reflecting different theological perspectives on divine judgment and human accountability. In 2 Samuel 24, God's judgment is portrayed as a direct response to David's pride and disobedience, highlighting the importance of humility and submission to God's will. In 1 Chronicles 21, Satan serves as a catalyst for David's sinful actions, emphasizing the role of spiritual warfare and the deceptive influence of evil forces.

3. Historical Considerations: Some scholars propose that the differences between 2 Samuel 24 and 1 Chronicles 21 may be attributed to variations in historical sources or editorial decisions within the biblical text. These variations could reflect different traditions or perspectives on the events surrounding David's census, resulting in nuanced portrayals of his reign and God's response to his actions.

Summary and Reflection:

The accounts of David's census in 2 Samuel 24 and 1 Chronicles 21 offer valuable insights into the dynamics of leadership, the consequences of sin, and the nature of divine judgment. Despite the apparent discrepancies between the narratives, they converge in highlighting the central theme of God's sovereignty and human accountability.

The contrasting perspectives presented in these accounts serve to deepen our understanding of David's reign and the complexities of divine-human interaction. Ultimately, they prompt reflection on the importance of humility, obedience, and trust in God's providence, even in the face of uncertainty and adversity.

6. David's Succession to the Throne

Scripture References:
- 2 Samuel 5:4-5
- 1 Chronicles 11:1-3

<u>Analysis</u>

The supposed contradiction in David's succession to the throne lies in the duration of his reign before Hebron. Here's a breakdown of the difference:

2 Samuel 5:4:

States David became king in Hebron and ruled over Judah for seven and a half years.

1 Chronicles 11:4:

Mentions David reigned over Judah in Hebron for two and a half years.

The discrepancy lies in the length of David's reign in Hebron before he became king over all Israel.

Context:

David's accession to the throne of Israel is a pivotal moment in the nation's history, marking the establishment of a unified monarchy under his leadership. The context surrounding David's succession includes the demise of Saul, the previous king, and the subsequent division and turmoil within Israel. David's ascent to the throne represents a culmination of divine promises and human actions, reflecting both God's providential guidance and David's courage and faith.

Language:

The language used in 2 Samuel 5 and 1 Chronicles 11 to describe David's coronation emphasizes his anointing and recognition as king over all Israel. Both accounts underscore David's divine appointment and the support he receives from the people of Israel and the elders of Judah. The choice of language highlights David's legitimacy as king and the unity of the nation under his rule.

Historical Background:

David's succession to the throne occurs against the backdrop of political and military challenges facing Israel. Following Saul's death, the nation experienced internal strife and external threats from neighboring enemies.

David's leadership was crucial in consolidating the tribes of Israel and establishing Jerusalem as the capital city. The historical context sheds light on the significance of David's reign and the challenges he faced as he sought to unify and strengthen the kingdom.

Theological Considerations:

From a theological perspective, David's accession to the throne is viewed as part of God's sovereign plan for Israel. Throughout the biblical narrative, God's hand is evident in guiding David's rise to power and shaping the destiny of the nation.

David's faithfulness and obedience to God's commands play a central role in his selection as king and his subsequent success in ruling over Israel. The theological significance of David's reign extends beyond mere political leadership to embodying the ideals of righteousness, justice, and covenant fidelity.

Insights from Scholars, Theologians, and Apologists

<u>Various Interpretations and Perspectives:</u>

1. Historical Context Analysis:

- Biblical scholars delve into the historical context surrounding David's ascent to the throne, examining factors such as the political landscape of ancient Israel, the aftermath of Saul's reign, and the socio-economic dynamics of the time. By situating the narratives within their historical milieu, scholars provide valuable insights into the challenges and opportunities facing David as he assumes leadership over the nation.

2. Literary and Theological Analysis:

- Theological scholars explore the literary and theological themes embedded in the narratives of David's succession, including divine providence, covenant fidelity, and the role of human agency. They examine the portrayal of David as a flawed yet chosen instrument of God, highlighting the tension between divine sovereignty and human responsibility in biblical history.

3. Comparative Studies:

- Apologists and comparative theologians conduct comparative studies between the narratives of David's succession in the books of Samuel and

Chronicles, identifying similarities and differences in their presentation. They analyze variations in language, structure, and emphasis, seeking to elucidate the theological significance of these textual differences and their implications for biblical interpretation.

4. Interdisciplinary Perspectives:

- Scholars from diverse disciplines, including archaeology, anthropology, and literary criticism, contribute interdisciplinary perspectives to the study of David's succession. They draw on archaeological evidence, comparative mythology, and textual analysis to contextualize the narratives within the broader cultural and intellectual milieu of the ancient Near East, enriching our understanding of David's historical legacy and cultural significance.

5. Hermeneutical Reflections:

- Theological hermeneutics scholars reflect on the interpretive methodologies employed in reading and interpreting the narratives of David's succession. They explore questions of textual criticism, literary genre, and theological interpretation, offering insights into the complexities of biblical exegesis and the challenges of reconciling apparent discrepancies within the biblical text.

Through their rigorous scholarship, theologians, apologists, and biblical scholars contribute valuable insights into the narratives of David's succession, shedding light on the theological, historical, and literary dimensions of these foundational texts. Their diverse perspectives enrich our understanding of David's role in Israel's history and his enduring significance as a figure of faith and leadership in the Judeo-Christian tradition.

Summary and Reflection:

The accounts of David's succession to the throne in 2 Samuel 5 and 1 Chronicles 11 offer valuable insights into the complexities of biblical kingship and divine providence. Despite differences in emphasis and detail, both narratives converge in affirming David's anointing as king and his pivotal role in shaping the destiny of Israel. As modern readers, we are invited to reflect on the enduring significance of David's reign and the timeless truths found in these ancient texts.

7. The Genealogy of King Saul

Scripture References:

- 1 Samuel 9:1-2
- 1 Chronicles 8:33-40

<u>Analysis</u>

The supposed contradiction lies in the father of Kish, King Saul's father.

1 Samuel 9:1

This passage introduces Kish as the son of Abiel: "Now there was a man of Benjamin, whose name was Kish, the son of Abiel, the son of Zeror, the son of Bechorath, the son of Aphiah, a Benjamite, a mighty man of valor."

1 Chronicles 8:33

While here it presents a different lineage, stating Kish's father as Ner: "Ner was the father of Kish, Kish the father of Saul, and Saul the father of Jonathan, Malki-Shua, Abinadab, and Esh-Baal."

This difference creates confusion: Was Kish's father Abiel or Ner?

Context:

In 1 Samuel 9, the genealogy of King Saul is briefly mentioned in the narrative, tracing his lineage back to Kish, his father. This passage primarily focuses on Saul's encounter with the prophet Samuel and his anointing as the first king of Israel. In contrast, 1 Chronicles 8 provides a more detailed genealogy of the tribe of Benjamin, which includes Saul as one of its prominent figures.

Language:

The language used in both passages is consistent with genealogical records found throughout the Old Testament. Names are listed in a linear fashion, often with brief descriptions or mentions of notable events associated with specific individuals. While 1 Samuel 9 provides a concise overview of Saul's lineage, 1 Chronicles 8 offers a more comprehensive genealogy of the tribe of Benjamin, of which Saul was a member.

Historical Background:

The historical background of Saul's genealogy is rooted in the tribal history of Israel, particularly the tribe of Benjamin. Saul's lineage is presented within the broader context of Israel's tribal identities and their significance in the nation's history. Understanding the historical context helps illuminate the purpose and significance of recording genealogies in ancient Israel, which often served political, religious, and social functions.

Theological Considerations:

From a theological perspective, the genealogies of Saul in 1 Samuel 9 and 1 Chronicles 8 emphasize the continuity of Israel's history and the fulfillment of God's promises to the patriarchs.

Despite variations in detail and emphasis, both genealogies affirm Saul's position as a descendant of Benjamin and a key figure in Israel's monarchy. The inclusion of Saul's genealogy in the biblical narrative underscores the divine sovereignty at work in Israel's history, as God orchestrates events according to His purposes.

Insights from Scholars, Theologians, and Apologists

<u>Various Interpretations and Perspectives:</u>

1. Complementary Genealogies: Some interpreters view the genealogies of Saul in 1 Samuel 9 and 1 Chronicles 8 as complementary rather than contradictory. While 1 Samuel 9 provides a brief overview of Saul's lineage within the context of the narrative, 1 Chronicles 8 offers a more detailed genealogy of the tribe of Benjamin, which includes Saul as one of its notable descendants.

2. Selective Emphasis: Others suggest that the differences between the two genealogies reflect the selective emphasis of the respective authors. The author of 1 Samuel may have focused on Saul's immediate ancestry to provide context for his introduction in the narrative, while the Chronicler in 1 Chronicles may have been more concerned with tracing the broader lineage of Benjamin.

3. Textual Transmission: Some scholars propose that variations between the genealogies may be attributed to differences in textual transmission or editorial decisions in compiling the biblical texts. These variations do not necessarily indicate contradictions but may reflect different sources or traditions utilized by the authors.

4. Historical Analysis: Scholars provide historical context to elucidate the purpose of genealogies in ancient Israel. They highlight how genealogies served

to establish legitimacy, trace lineage, and preserve tribal identities. Understanding the cultural and political dynamics of ancient Israel sheds light on why different genealogical records may emphasize certain details or lineages.

5. Literary Criticism: Theological scholars employ literary criticism to analyze the textual differences between 1 Samuel 9 and 1 Chronicles 8. They explore the genre, style, and narrative intentions of each book to discern why variations exist. This approach helps reconcile apparent discrepancies by recognizing the diverse literary techniques and editorial decisions employed by the biblical authors.

6. Theological Reflection: Theologians delve into the theological implications of Saul's genealogy, considering its significance within the broader biblical narrative. They emphasize theological themes such as God's sovereignty, covenant faithfulness, and the role of human agency in fulfilling divine purposes. By examining the theological motifs embedded within the genealogies, theologians offer deeper insights into the overarching narrative of redemption woven throughout Scripture.

7. Comparative Analysis: Apologists engage in comparative analysis to reconcile differences between the genealogies in 1 Samuel 9 and 1 Chronicles 8. They compare parallel passages, cross-reference related texts, and consult historical sources to construct a harmonized understanding of Saul's lineage. Through meticulous study and synthesis of biblical and extra biblical evidence, apologists demonstrate the coherence of Scripture and address potential objections to its reliability.

8. Textual Criticism: Scholars of textual criticism investigate variant readings and manuscript traditions to ascertain the original wording of the biblical texts. They evaluate textual variants within the genealogies of King Saul to determine the most accurate representation of the original manuscripts. By applying rigorous textual analysis, scholars contribute to the scholarly consensus on the reliability and integrity of biblical transmission.

9. Synthesis of Perspectives: Integrating diverse perspectives, scholars, theologians, and apologists offer a holistic understanding of Saul's genealogy. They emphasize the multidisciplinary approach required to interpret complex biblical passages, acknowledging the interplay between historical, literary, theological, and textual factors. By synthesizing various insights, scholars

provide comprehensive explanations that elucidate the nuances of Saul's lineage and its significance within the broader biblical narrative.

Summary and Reflection:

The genealogies of King Saul in 1 Samuel 9 and 1 Chronicles 8 contribute to our understanding of Israel's tribal history and the establishment of the monarchy. While these passages may differ in detail and emphasis, they converge in affirming Saul's position as a descendant of Benjamin and a key figure in Israel's history. Through careful study and interpretation, we gain deeper insights into the continuity of God's redemptive plan and the unfolding of His purposes in the history of Israel.

8. The Rebuilding of the Temple

Scripture References:

- Ezra 3:8-13
- Ezra 5:1-2, 6-17
- Ezra 6:1-15

<u>Analysis</u>

The supposed contradiction in the rebuilding of the temple between Ezra 3 and Ezra 5-6 lies in the timing and authorization of the project. Here's a breakdown:

Ezra 3:

* Describes the Israelites returning exiles who gathered in Jerusalem (around 538 BC).

* They laid the foundation of the temple "in the first year of their coming..." (Ezra 3:2).

* This suggests they began rebuilding the temple independently, without documented permission from a governing authority.

Ezra 5-6:

* Introduces a decree by Darius I (dated around 520 BC) that officially authorizes the rebuilding of the temple (Ezra 6:6-7).

* This seems to contradict the idea that construction already began in Ezra 3.

Therefore, it seems the contradiction lies in the sequence of events and authorization for the temple's reconstruction.

Context:

Ezra 3 narrates the early stages of the temple's reconstruction upon the return of the Jewish exiles to Jerusalem after their captivity in Babylon. The focus is on the spiritual restoration and renewal of worship practices, with an emphasis on laying the foundation of the temple. However, in Ezra 5-6, the narrative shifts to the challenges faced during the rebuilding process, including opposition from neighboring peoples and political intervention from the Persian authorities.

Language:

In Ezra 3, the language exudes enthusiasm and celebration as the people initiate the rebuilding process. It underscores their dedication to restoring the worship of Yahweh and the joy they experience in laying the foundation of the temple. Conversely, Ezra 5-6 employs legalistic language, detailing the formal complaints lodged against the Jewish community by their adversaries and the subsequent investigations conducted by the Persian officials.

Historical Background:

The events described in Ezra occurred during the Persian period when Cyrus the Great issued a decree allowing the Jewish exiles to return to Jerusalem and rebuild the temple. The rebuilding efforts faced opposition from neighboring peoples, leading to delays and complications in the reconstruction process. However, under the reign of King Darius, the temple project was ultimately completed with the support of the Persian authorities.

Theological Considerations:

The rebuilding of the temple held immense theological significance for the Jewish people, symbolizing God's faithfulness in restoring His covenant relationship with His chosen people. Despite the challenges and setbacks faced during the rebuilding process, the completion of the temple underscored God's sovereignty over history and His commitment to fulfilling His promises to His people.

Insights from Scholars, Theologians, and Apologists

<u>Various Interpretations and Perspectives:</u>

1. Historical Context:

Scholars emphasize the importance of understanding the historical context surrounding the events described in Ezra 3 and Ezra 5-6. The rebuilding of the temple occurred during the Persian period, following the decree of Cyrus the Great allowing the Jewish exiles to return to Jerusalem. This historical backdrop informs interpretations of the challenges and opposition faced by the Jewish community during the reconstruction efforts.

2. Literary Analysis:

The differences in language and style between Ezra 3 and Ezra 5-6 reflect distinct literary purposes and perspectives. Ezra 3 focuses on the spiritual renewal and communal celebration surrounding the laying of the temple's foundation. In contrast, Ezra 5-6 adopt a more formal and legalistic tone, detailing the complaints raised by adversaries and the subsequent investigations by Persian officials. Scholars highlight the importance of literary analysis in discerning the intended meanings and emphases of each passage.

3. Theological Significance:

The theological implications of the temple's reconstruction are central to interpretations of Ezra 3 and Ezra 5-6. The completion of the temple symbolizes God's faithfulness in restoring His covenant relationship with His people and the renewal of worship practices. The challenges faced by the Jewish community underscore the ongoing struggle between fidelity to Yahweh and opposition from external forces. Scholars and theologians explore the theological themes of perseverance, divine providence, and covenant faithfulness evident in these passages.

4. Legal and Political Dynamics:

Apologists delve into the legal and political dynamics depicted in Ezra 5-6, analyzing the interactions between the Jewish community and the Persian authorities. The formal complaints lodged against the Jews by their adversaries raise questions about religious freedom and the exercise of authority within the Persian Empire. Apologists highlight the role of King Darius in upholding Cyrus's decree and ensuring the completion of the temple despite opposition from vested interests.

5. Harmonization and Interpretive Strategies:

The apparent differences between Ezra 3 and Ezra 5-6 prompt scholars and theologians to employ various harmonization and interpretive strategies. Some advocate for a complementary approach, viewing the passages as offering different perspectives on the temple's reconstruction. Others emphasize the symbolic and theological significance of the events, interpreting them within the broader narrative of Israel's restoration and redemption. Apologists engage with critical questions raised by skeptics regarding the historical accuracy and reliability of the biblical accounts, offering reasoned defenses of the text's integrity.

Overall, insights from scholars, theologians, and apologists enrich our understanding of the complexities surrounding the temple's reconstruction in Ezra 3 and Ezra 5-6. Their analyses shed light on the historical, literary, theological, and apologetic dimensions of these passages, demonstrating the enduring relevance of biblical scholarship in interpreting and applying Scripture.

Summary and Reflection:

While Ezra 3 and Ezra 5-6 may present different emphases and levels of detail, they ultimately converge in affirming God's providential care and faithfulness in the restoration of His people and the reconstruction of the temple. These passages testify to the perseverance of the Jewish community in the face of opposition and adversity, as well as God's sovereign intervention in fulfilling His purposes through history.

9. The Death of Goliath

Scripture References:
- 1 Samuel 17
- 2 Samuel 21:19

<u>Analysis</u>

The supposed contradiction lies in who kills Goliath.

1 Samuel 17:

Tells the story of David defeating Goliath in a famous duel. David uses a slingshot and a stone to strike Goliath down.

2 Samuel 21:19:

Mentions Goliath again, but this time it says Elhanan, the son of Jaare-Oregim, killed Goliath.

This difference creates confusion: Did David or Elhanan kill Goliath?

Context:

In 1 Samuel 17, the well-known narrative of David and Goliath unfolds during the reign of King Saul. Goliath, a champion of the Philistine army, challenges the Israelites to send a champion to fight him. David, a young shepherd boy, volunteers to confront Goliath and defeats him with a sling and a stone. This victory catapults David to fame and eventually leads to his rise as a hero in Israel.

In 2 Samuel 21:19, a brief mention is made of another encounter between David and a Philistine giant named "Ishbi-benob." The passage recounts how "Elhanan the son of Jaare-oregim, the Bethlehemite, struck him down" but does not explicitly mention Goliath.

Language:

The language in 1 Samuel 17 vividly describes the confrontation between David and Goliath, emphasizing the dramatic nature of the event and its significance in David's rise to prominence. The narrative portrays Goliath as a formidable foe and highlights David's courage and reliance on God to achieve victory.

In 2 Samuel 21:19, the mention of "Ishbi-benob" as the giant slain by Elhanan is brief and lacks the detail and prominence given to the encounter between David and Goliath in 1 Samuel 17.

Historical Background:

The historical context of 1 Samuel 17 places the confrontation between David and Goliath within the broader context of the ongoing conflict between the Israelites and the Philistines. This battle occurs during the early period of Saul's reign as king of Israel and serves as a pivotal moment in David's emergence as a key figure in Israelite history.

The historical background of 2 Samuel 21:19 is less detailed, and the encounter between Elhanan and "Ishbi-benob" is mentioned in passing without providing extensive historical context.

Theological Considerations:

The theological significance of David's victory over Goliath in 1 Samuel 17 is multifaceted. It underscores themes of faith, courage, and divine intervention, demonstrating God's sovereignty in delivering His people from their enemies and fulfilling His purposes through unlikely heroes like David.

While the encounter between Elhanan and "Ishbi-benob" in 2 Samuel 21:19 may not carry the same theological weight as the story of David and Goliath, it still serves as a reminder of God's faithfulness in granting victory to His people in times of conflict.

Insights from Scholars, Theologians, and Apologists

<u>Various Interpretations and Perspectives:</u>

1. Textual Analysis:

Scholars delve into the textual nuances of 1 Samuel 17 and 2 Samuel 21:19 to understand the differences in language, style, and context between the two passages. They examine factors such as manuscript variations, literary conventions, and editorial decisions that may contribute to variations in the portrayal of events and characters.

2. Historical Context:

Theological historians and biblical archaeologists provide insights into the historical context of ancient Israel and its interactions with neighboring peoples such as the Philistines. They explore archaeological evidence, ancient inscriptions, and comparative studies of Near Eastern cultures to shed light on the historical accuracy and cultural significance of biblical narratives.

3. Theological Interpretation:

Theological scholars and exegetes analyze the theological themes and motifs present in the stories of David and Goliath and other biblical narratives.

They explore concepts such as divine providence, human agency, and theodicy to interpret the significance of these events within the broader framework of biblical theology.

4. Apologetic Perspectives:

Apologists address questions and objections raised by skeptics and critics regarding apparent contradictions in the Bible. They offer reasoned explanations, harmonization, and alternative interpretations to reconcile seemingly conflicting passages and demonstrate the coherence and reliability of Scripture.

5. Literary and Redactional Analysis:

Scholars of biblical literature and redaction criticism examine the literary structure, composition, and editorial history of biblical texts to discern the intentions of the authors and editors responsible for their final form. They identify patterns of repetition, variation, and thematic development that may account for differences between parallel accounts in the Bible.

6. Comparative Studies:

Comparative theologians and scholars of comparative religion explore parallels and similarities between biblical narratives and stories found in other religious traditions and cultural contexts. They analyze cross-cultural motifs, archetypes, and motifs to enrich our understanding of biblical storytelling and its universal themes.

7. Community Traditions:

Scholars of Jewish and Christian traditions examine the ways in which different religious communities interpret and transmit biblical narratives through oral tradition, liturgical practice, and theological reflection. They explore how diverse religious communities engage with and interpret biblical stories to shape their collective identity and faith practice.

8. Contemporary Relevance:

Theological ethicists and contemporary theologians reflect on the relevance of biblical narratives such as David and Goliath for contemporary ethical dilemmas and social justice issues. They draw connections between biblical themes of justice, mercy, and solidarity and contemporary challenges facing individuals and communities today.

Summary and Reflection:

The apparent contradiction between 1 Samuel 17 and 2 Samuel 21:19 regarding the death of Goliath invites careful examination and interpretation of the biblical text. While both passages describe encounters between Israelites and Philistine warriors, they may represent distinct events or perspectives within Israel's history. Understanding the nuances of these narratives enriches our appreciation for the multifaceted nature of biblical storytelling and the theological themes it conveys.

10. The Duration of Solomon's Reign

Scripture References:

1 Kings 4:25

2 Chronicles 9:30

<u>Analysis</u>

The supposed contradiction in the Bible lies in the length of Solomon's reign. Here's the breakdown:

<u>*1 Kings 4:21:*</u>

States that Solomon "reigned over all Israel forty years." (NIV)

<u>*2 Chronicles 9:30:*</u>

Mentions that Solomon reigned in Jerusalem over all Israel "forty years." (NIV)

The difference seems minor, but some argue it's a contradiction. Here's why:

Context:

In 1 Kings 4 and 2 Chronicles 9, the duration of Solomon's reign is recorded differently. 1 Kings 4:25 states that Solomon reigned over Israel for forty years, while 2 Chronicles 9:30 indicates that Solomon's reign lasted for forty years in total.

Language:

Both passages use clear and straightforward language to convey the duration of Solomon's reign. However, the discrepancy arises from whether the reign was inclusive of the time Solomon ruled over both Israel and Judah or solely over Judah.

Historical Background:

To understand the difference between the two accounts, it's essential to consider the historical context of Israel and Judah during Solomon's reign. Solomon initially ruled over the united kingdom of Israel and Judah, but after his death, the kingdom split into two separate entities. Therefore, the duration of his reign may be calculated differently depending on whether it includes the time he ruled over both kingdoms or just one.

Theological Considerations:

The differing accounts of Solomon's reign raise theological questions about the reliability and interpretation of biblical narratives. While both passages aim to convey historical facts, they may prioritize different aspects of Solomon's reign or interpret the chronology differently based on their theological purposes.

Insights from Scholars, Theologians, and Apologists
<u>Various Interpretations and Perspectives:</u>

1. Inclusive vs. Exclusive Calculation: Some scholars interpret 1 Kings 4:25 as including the entirety of Solomon's reign, including his rule over both Israel and Judah, while 2 Chronicles 9:30 may focus exclusively on his reign over Judah. This interpretation reconciles the apparent contradiction by considering different perspectives on the duration of Solomon's reign.

2. Editorial Emphasis: Others suggest that the differences in the duration of Solomon's reign reflect editorial choices made by the authors or redactors of 1 Kings and 2 Chronicles. These differences may stem from theological or literary concerns rather than discrepancies in historical fact.

3. Harmonization: Some theologians harmonize the two accounts by proposing alternative explanations for the discrepancy. For example, they may suggest that the forty-year duration mentioned in 1 Kings 4:25 includes the time Solomon co-reigned with his father David, whereas the forty-year duration in 2 Chronicles 9:30 refers specifically to Solomon's sole reign over Judah.

4. Historical Context: Scholars emphasize the importance of understanding the historical context of Israel and Judah during Solomon's reign. This includes considering factors such as the division of the kingdom after Solomon's death and the different perspectives of the authors of 1 Kings and 2 Chronicles.

5. Textual Analysis: Theologians delve into the nuances of the Hebrew text and the wording used in 1 Kings 4:25 and 2 Chronicles 9:30. They explore whether the discrepancy arises from variations in terminology or editorial choices made by the authors or redactors.

6. Theological Interpretation: Apologists offer theological perspectives on the purpose of the differing accounts. They consider whether the emphasis of each passage aligns with theological themes or literary conventions prevalent in their respective books.

7. Harmonization Techniques: Some scholars propose harmonization methods to reconcile the contradiction. This includes suggesting that one account may include the time Solomon co-reigned with his father David, while the other specifies only the duration of Solomon's sole reign over Judah.

8. Literary Analysis: Theological scholars analyze the literary structure and theological themes of 1 Kings and 2 Chronicles. They explore whether the differences in the duration of Solomon's reign serve a broader narrative or theological purpose within each book.

9. Historical Accuracy: Apologists address questions regarding the historical accuracy of biblical narratives. They examine whether the discrepancy in the duration of Solomon's reign reflects variations in historical records, editorial decisions, or theological emphases.

Summary and Reflection:

The difference in the duration of Solomon's reign between 1 Kings 4:25 and 2 Chronicles 9:30 underscores the complexities of interpreting biblical chronology and historical narratives. While the passages aim to convey factual information about Solomon's reign, they may emphasize different aspects or calculate the duration differently based on their respective contexts and theological purposes. Ultimately, grappling with apparent contradictions such as this prompts readers to engage more deeply with the biblical text, its historical background, and its theological implications.

11. The Number of David's Mighty Men

Scripture References:

2 Samuel 23:8-39

1 Chronicles 11:10-47

<u>Analysis</u>

The supposed contradiction here lies in the number and names of David's mightiest warriors.

2 Samuel 23:

This chapter introduces David's "mighty men" and highlights three "the thirty" warriors, with the first one being Jashobeam, a Hachmonite, who slew 800 men at one time (v. 8).

1 Chronicles 11:

This chapter also presents David's "mighty men," but the number "thirty" is not mentioned. Here, Jashobeam, a Tachmonite (slight variation in name), is identified as the chief of the "thirty," but the number slain is only 300 (v. 11).

There are two main points of difference:

1. Number of "Thirty" Warriors: 2 Samuel mentions "the thirty" while 1 Chronicles doesn't explicitly use that term.

2. Number Slain by Jashobeam: 2 Samuel credits Jashobeam with killing 800, while 1 Chronicles says 300.

Context:

In both 2 Samuel 23 and 1 Chronicles 11, we find accounts of David's mighty men, a group of elite warriors who served alongside him. These men were renowned for their courage, loyalty, and valor in battle. While 2 Samuel 23 provides a detailed list of these mighty men and their individual feats, 1 Chronicles 11 offers a similar account but with variations in the list and descriptions of their accomplishments.

Language:

The language used in both passages portrays David's mighty men as fearless warriors who fought valiantly for their king and kingdom. Their exploits are described in vivid detail, highlighting their extraordinary bravery and dedication. While there may be differences in wording and phrasing between the two accounts, the overarching portrayal of these mighty men remains consistent.

Historical Background:

Understanding the historical context of David's reign and military campaigns helps shed light on the composition and achievements of his mighty men. These warriors played a crucial role in securing David's kingdom and defending it against external threats. Variations in the lists and descriptions of mighty men may be attributed to differences in available sources, oral traditions, or regional variations in historical records.

Theological Considerations:

Both passages emphasize the significance of David's mighty men in Israelite history and the establishment of David's kingdom. Their courage, loyalty, and prowess in battle are presented as attributes that contributed to the success of David's reign. The narratives also underscore the role of divine assistance in empowering David and his warriors for victory.

Insights from Scholars, Theologians, and Apologists

Various Interpretations and Perspectives:

1. Historical Context: Scholars emphasize the historical context of David's reign, considering factors such as changes in military personnel over time, variations in troop sizes, and the challenges of accurately recording historical data in ancient texts.

2. Textual Analysis: Theologians delve into the wording and structure of the passages in 2 Samuel 23 and 1 Chronicles 11. They explore whether differences in numbers are the result of textual variants, editorial decisions, or the use of different sources by the authors.

3. Theological Interpretation: Apologists consider the theological significance of the accounts of David's mighty men within the broader narrative of Israelite history. They highlight themes of courage, loyalty, and divine providence, regardless of specific numerical discrepancies.

4. Harmonization Techniques: Some scholars propose harmonization methods to reconcile the apparent contradiction. This may include considering whether one account includes honorary titles or whether certain individuals

served in multiple capacities, leading to variations in the total number of mighty men listed.

5. Literary Analysis: Theological scholars analyze the literary structure and themes of 2 Samuel and 1 Chronicles. They explore whether differences in the numbers of mighty men serve a broader narrative or theological purpose within each book, such as emphasizing David's military prowess or highlighting the importance of his closest companions.

6. Historical Accuracy: Apologists address questions about the historical accuracy of biblical narratives, acknowledging the challenges of interpreting ancient texts. They emphasize the need to approach discrepancies with humility, recognizing the limitations of human understanding and the complexity of historical recording.

Summary and Reflection:

Despite the variations between the accounts in 2 Samuel 23 and 1 Chronicles 11 regarding the number and descriptions of David's mighty men, both passages highlight the central role of these warriors in the establishment and defense of David's kingdom. The differences between the lists and descriptions may be attributed to various factors, including differences in sources, editorial decisions, or the specific focus of each narrative. Nonetheless, the overarching portrayal of David's mighty men as courageous and loyal servants of their king and God remains unchanged.

12. Tribe of Ephraim

Scripture References:
- Judges 1:19
- Joshua 17:18

<u>Analysis</u>

You've identified an interesting difference between Judges 1:19 and Joshua 17:18. Let's explore why this isn't necessarily a contradiction:

<u>Judges 1:19</u>

Here, it says, "So the Lord was with Judah. And they drove out the mountaineers, but they could not drive out the inhabitants of the lowland, because they had chariots of iron." This verse describes the tribe of Judah's conquest and specifies their struggle against the Canaanites in the lowlands who had iron chariots.

<u>Joshua 17:18</u>

This verse states, "But the mountain country shall be yours. Although it is wooded, you shall cut it down, and its farthest extent shall be yours; for you shall drive out the Canaanites, though they have iron chariots and are strong." This is part of Joshua's instructions to the descendants of Joseph (which includes Ephraim) as they prepare to inherit their land. Here, it seems to promise victory over the Canaanites despite their chariots.

Judges 1:19 states that the tribe of Ephraim did not drive out the Canaanites, while Joshua 17:18 suggests they were unable to drive them out due to the Canaanites' superior military power.

Context:

In Judges 1:19, after the death of Joshua, the tribes of Israel continued the conquest of Canaan. The tribe of Ephraim failed to fully drive out the Canaanites from their allotted territory. In Joshua 17:18, Joshua addresses the tribe of Ephraim, acknowledging their complaint about the mountainous region they were allotted.

He advises them to clear the forested land, indicating that although they had the capacity to drive out the Canaanites, they had not fully done so. The accounts in Judges and Joshua highlight the incomplete conquest of Canaan by the Israelites, particularly the tribe of Ephraim. While Judges 1:19 directly states that Ephraim did not drive out the Canaanites, Joshua 17:18 implies that they were capable but failed to do so completely.

Language:

In Judges 1:19, the language is straightforward, stating that the tribe of Ephraim did not drive out the Canaanites. In Joshua 17:18, Joshua encourages Ephraim to clear the land themselves, suggesting they had the ability to drive out the Canaanites but had not yet done so.

Historical Background:

The conquest of Canaan was a complex and gradual process that unfolded over several generations. While the Israelites experienced military victories, they also faced challenges and resistance from the Canaanite inhabitants. The tribe of Ephraim's failure to fully drive out the Canaanites may have been influenced by various factors, including the terrain, the strength of Canaanite fortifications, and internal divisions among the Israelites.

Theological Considerations:

The incomplete conquest of Canaan underscores theological themes such as the Israelites' obedience to God's commands, the consequences of disobedience, and the ongoing struggle between faithfulness and compromise. The failure of Ephraim to fully drive out the Canaanites serves as a cautionary tale about the dangers of compromise and the need for wholehearted obedience to God's instructions.

Insights from Scholars, Theologians, and Apologists

<u>Various Interpretations and Perspectives</u>:

Interpreters offer different perspectives on the reasons for Ephraim's failure to drive out the Canaanites. Some view it as a lack of faith or commitment on the part of the tribe, while others emphasize external factors such as military challenges or strategic considerations. Some scholars also suggest that the accounts in Judges and Joshua may reflect different stages of the conquest or variations in oral traditions.

1. Historical Context and Archaeological Evidence: Scholars consider the historical context of the Israelite conquest of Canaan, examining archaeological evidence and ancient Near Eastern texts to understand the complexities of this period. They recognize that the conquest was not a single event but a gradual

process spanning generations, characterized by both military campaigns and periods of coexistence with the Canaanite inhabitants. This nuanced perspective helps contextualize the challenges faced by individual tribes like Ephraim in fully occupying their allotted territories.

2. Textual Analysis and Literary Criticism: Theological scholars employ textual analysis and literary criticism to explore the nuances of the passages in Judges and Joshua. They examine the language, style, and narrative structure of these texts, considering factors such as editorial redaction, literary genre, and theological emphasis. By understanding the distinct literary conventions and theological purposes of Judges and Joshua, scholars gain insights into the differing portrayals of Ephraim's conquest efforts.

3. Theological Themes and Moral Lessons: Theological reflections on the conquest of Canaan emphasize broader themes such as obedience to God's commands, the consequences of disobedience, and the tension between divine sovereignty and human agency. Scholars highlight the moral lessons embedded in the narratives, including the dangers of compromise, the importance of faithfulness in fulfilling God's purposes, and the need for repentance and renewal in the face of failure.

4. Redemptive-Historical Perspective: Apologists and theologians often approach the Old Testament narratives from a redemptive-historical perspective, interpreting them within the broader framework of God's unfolding plan of salvation. They view the conquest of Canaan as part of God's covenant promises to Israel, ultimately pointing forward to the coming of Christ and the establishment of His kingdom. This perspective helps readers see how the experiences of ancient Israel foreshadow spiritual truths and principles applicable to believers today.

5. Interpretive Challenges and Humility: Scholars acknowledge the interpretive challenges posed by passages like Judges 1:19 and Joshua 17:18, recognizing that some details may remain ambiguous or subject to varying interpretations. They emphasize the importance of humility in grappling with difficult passages, recognizing that our understanding is finite and may be influenced by cultural, linguistic, and theological biases. This posture of humility fosters a spirit of openness to continued study, dialogue, and growth in understanding.

Summary and Reflection:

The supposed contradiction regarding the conquest of Canaan by the tribe of Ephraim reflects the complexities of interpreting historical narratives in the Bible. Rather than viewing it as a discrepancy, it invites readers to consider the various factors at play and the theological lessons embedded in the text. Ultimately, the accounts in Judges and Joshua highlight the ongoing struggle of God's people to remain faithful to His commands amidst challenges and obstacles.

13. Genealogies of Jesus

Scripture References:
- Matthew 1:1-17
- Luke 3:23-38

<u>Analysis</u>

The supposed contradiction in the Bible lies in the genealogies of Jesus presented in the Gospels of:

Matthew 1: This genealogy traces Jesus' lineage through Joseph, his adoptive father. It starts with Abraham and goes through King David, then to Jesus.

Luke 3: This genealogy traces Jesus' lineage through Mary, his biological mother. It starts with God and goes through David, then to Jesus.

There are two main differences that create the contradiction:

1. Ancestral Line: Matthew and Luke trace Jesus' lineage through different parents (Joseph vs. Mary).

2. Listed Ancestors: The names listed between David and Jesus differ in the two Gospels.

Context:

The genealogies of Jesus presented in the Gospels of Matthew and Luke serve distinct purposes within the narratives of each Gospel. Matthew, writing to a primarily Jewish audience, emphasizes Jesus' connection to the Davidic lineage, fulfilling Messianic prophecies found in the Hebrew Scriptures. In contrast, Luke, writing to a broader audience, highlights Jesus' universal mission and His identity as the Son of Man, tracing His lineage back to Adam, the progenitor of all humanity.

Language:

Matthew's genealogy is structured into three sets of fourteen generations, likely for mnemonic purposes, emphasizing key figures in Israel's history. This structure underscores Jesus' continuity with Israel's past and positions Him as the culmination of God's redemptive plan. Luke's genealogy, while more extensive, lacks the same structured format but traces Jesus' ancestry through a different lineage, possibly that of Mary or a maternal ancestor, highlighting His connection to all humanity.

Historical Background:

Genealogies held significant importance in ancient Jewish culture, serving to establish legitimacy, inheritance rights, and social status. Matthew's genealogy underscores Jesus' legal right to the Davidic throne through His legal father, Joseph, while Luke's genealogy may emphasize Jesus' physical descent from Adam, emphasizing His universal role as the Savior of humanity.

Theological Considerations:

Both genealogies contribute to the theological portrait of Jesus presented in the Gospels. Matthew emphasizes Jesus' Messianic identity and fulfillment of Old Testament promises, emphasizing His role as the King of Israel. Luke, while also affirming Jesus' Messianic credentials, emphasizes His humanity and His solidarity with all humanity as the Son of Man, the Second Adam who brings redemption to all.

Insights from Scholars, Theologians, and Apologists

<u>Various Interpretations and Perspectives:</u>

1. Legal vs. Biological Descent: Some scholars suggest that the differences between Matthew's and Luke's genealogies may be attributed to the legal and biological descent of Jesus. Matthew's genealogy, tracing Jesus' lineage through Joseph, emphasizes His legal right to the Davidic throne and the fulfillment of Messianic promises regarding the royal lineage. In contrast, Luke's genealogy, which may trace Jesus' lineage through Mary or a maternal ancestor, underscores His biological connection to humanity, highlighting His role as the Second Adam and the Savior of all.

2. Literary and Theological Devices: Other scholars interpret the differences between the genealogies as deliberate literary and theological devices employed by the Gospel writers. Matthew, writing to a Jewish audience, structures his genealogy into three sets of fourteen generations, emphasizing key figures in Israel's history and highlighting Jesus' continuity with Israel's past. Luke, writing to a broader audience, presents a more extensive genealogy that traces Jesus' ancestry back to Adam, emphasizing His universal significance and His solidarity with all humanity.

3. Theological Emphases: The differences between Matthew's and Luke's genealogies may reflect the distinct theological emphases of each Gospel. Matthew emphasizes Jesus' Messianic identity and His fulfillment of Old Testament prophecies, positioning Him as the promised King of Israel. Luke, while also affirming Jesus' Messianic credentials, emphasizes His universal mission and His role as the Savior of all humanity, tracing His lineage back to the common ancestor of humanity, Adam.

4. Historical Considerations: The differences between the genealogies may also be understood in light of historical and cultural factors. Genealogies served various purposes in ancient Jewish culture, including establishing legitimacy, inheritance rights, and social status. Matthew's genealogy emphasizes Jesus' legal right to the Davidic throne through Joseph, while Luke's genealogy may highlight His biological descent from Adam, emphasizing His universal significance and His connection to all humanity.

Scholars, theologians, and apologists offer various perspectives and interpretations to reconcile the differences between Matthew's and Luke's genealogies of Jesus. They recognize the richness and complexity of the genealogies of Jesus. While there may be differences in the details and structures of the genealogies, they ultimately contribute to our understanding of Jesus' identity, mission, and significance within the overarching narrative of Scripture. These explanations may vary, but they affirm the theological significance of Jesus' lineage and His fulfillment of Old Testament prophecies.

Summary and Reflection:

Despite the apparent differences between Matthew's and Luke's genealogies of Jesus, both accounts contribute to our understanding of Jesus' identity, mission, and significance within the overarching narrative of Scripture. The complexities of these genealogies invite deeper reflection on the theological themes they convey and enrich our appreciation of Jesus' role as the Messiah and Savior of the world.

14. Jesus' Resurrection Appearances

Scripture References:
- Matthew 28:1-20
- Mark 16:1-20
- Luke 24:1-53
- John 20:1-31; 21:1-25

Analysis

The supposed contradiction lies in the details of Jesus' appearances to his disciples after the resurrection. Here's a breakdown of the variations across the four Gospels:

Gospel	Location of First Appearance	Women at the Tomb?	Jesus Appeared to Women?	Other Appearances
Matthew 28	Near the tomb	Mary Magdalene and the other Mary	Yes	To two disciples on the road
Mark 16	Not mentioned	Not mentioned	Optional ending mentions it	Not mentioned
Luke 24	On the road to Emmaus	Mary Magdalene	Yes, on the way back from Emmaus	To the disciples on the road to Emmaus, then later that evening to the disciples in Jerusalem
John 20-21	A locked room	Mary Magdalene	Yes	To the disciples multiple times, including one appearance with Thomas present

The discrepancies lie in:

Location of the first appearance:

Matthew and Luke mention different locations.

Women at the tomb: Mark doesn't mention the women, while the others do.

Mark 16: Some versions include additional verses describing Jesus' appearances, while others omit them.

Context:

The Gospels of Matthew, Mark, Luke, and John each provide accounts of Jesus' resurrection appearances to his disciples and followers. While there are similarities in the events described, each Gospel presents unique details and perspectives on the resurrection appearances. These variations have led to questions and debates among scholars and readers regarding the consistency of the accounts.

Language:

The language used in the resurrection narratives reflects the awe, astonishment, and joy experienced by the disciples upon encountering the risen Jesus. Each Gospel employs different literary styles and vocabularies to convey the emotions and reactions of the disciples as they witness the miraculous events surrounding the resurrection. Despite linguistic differences, the overarching message of Jesus' victory over death remains consistent across the accounts.

Historical Background:

Understanding the historical context of Jesus' resurrection is crucial for interpreting the Gospel narratives. The events took place within the broader context of first-century Judaism and the Roman Empire, amidst political tensions, religious expectations, and cultural norms of the time. Scholars consider factors such as eyewitness testimony, oral traditions, and early Christian communities when assessing the historical reliability of the resurrection accounts.

Theological Considerations:

The resurrection appearances hold profound theological significance for Christian faith and doctrine. They affirm Jesus' identity as the Son of God and the fulfillment of Old Testament prophecies concerning the Messiah. The resurrection validates Jesus' teachings, validates his victory over sin and death, and inaugurates the new covenant era of salvation. The theological themes of redemption, reconciliation, and the hope of eternal life are central to the resurrection narratives.

Insights from Scholars, Theologians, and Apologists <u>Various Interpretations and Perspectives:</u>

1. Harmonization of Accounts: Scholars often approach the resurrection narratives by harmonizing the accounts across the four Gospels. They recognize that each Gospel writer provides unique perspectives and details about the

events surrounding Jesus' resurrection appearances. By comparing and synthesizing these accounts, scholars aim to create a cohesive timeline of the resurrection events.

2. Differences in Emphasis: Theologians note that each Gospel writer emphasizes different aspects of the resurrection appearances based on their theological agendas and the needs of their respective audiences. For example, Matthew highlights the authority and commissioning of Jesus to his disciples, while John emphasizes themes of belief and restoration.

3. Variations in Detail: Apologists address apparent discrepancies in the details of the resurrection appearances, such as the number of women present at the empty tomb or the specific locations where Jesus appeared to his disciples. They explain that these variations may stem from differences in eyewitness testimonies, the order in which events occurred, or the inclusion of specific details for theological emphasis.

4. Literary and Theological Themes: Theological scholars analyze the literary and theological themes present in each Gospel's resurrection narrative. They explore how each Gospel writer's unique style, vocabulary, and theological perspective shape their portrayal of the resurrection appearances. For example, Mark's Gospel emphasizes the disciples' initial disbelief and fear, while Luke's Gospel focuses on Jesus' commissioning of his disciples to preach the gospel to all nations.

5. Historical Accuracy: Apologists defend the historical accuracy of the resurrection accounts by highlighting the reliability of the Gospel narratives as historical documents. They point to corroborating evidence from early Christian writings, archaeological discoveries, and extra-biblical sources that support the basic facts of Jesus' resurrection and post-resurrection appearances.

6. Theological Significance: Scholars and theologians emphasize the theological significance of Jesus' resurrection appearances as central to Christian faith and doctrine. They highlight how the resurrection validates Jesus' claims to be the Son of God and the Messiah, fulfills Old Testament prophecies, and inaugurates the new covenant era of salvation history.

In summary, it's important to remember that the Gospels are not intended to be strict historical biographies. They are theological accounts that emphasize the significance of Jesus' resurrection and its meaning for believers. Here are some additional points to consider:

* All four Gospels agree on the core message: Jesus died on the cross and rose again from the dead.

* The variations might reflect the different experiences of the women and disciples who encountered the resurrected Jesus.

* The details might be less important than the overall message of hope and new life brought about by the resurrection.

Summary and Reflection:

Despite differences in the resurrection narratives found in Matthew, Mark, Luke, and John, the overarching message of Jesus' victory over death and the hope of salvation is consistent. The variations in details and perspectives reflect the diverse eyewitness testimonies and theological emphases of the Gospel writers. Ultimately, the resurrection appearances attest to the transformative power of Christ's resurrection and its enduring impact on Christian faith and belief.

15. The Fate of Judas Iscariot

Scripture References:
- Matthew 27:3-10
- Acts 1:16-20

<u>Analysis</u>

The supposed contradiction here concerns the death of Judas Iscariot.

Matthew 27:3-10:

Describes Judas regretting his betrayal, returning the 30 silver pieces, and then hanging himself.

Acts 1:18:

Mentions Judas acquiring a field with the money he received for betraying Jesus, then falling headlong and his body bursting open.

The difference lies in the manner of death: hanging (Matthew) vs. falling and bodily rupture (Acts).

Context:

In Matthew 27 and Acts 1, we encounter accounts of the fate of Judas Iscariot following his betrayal of Jesus. Matthew's Gospel describes Judas' remorse and subsequent suicide by hanging, while Acts provides additional details about his death and the use of the money he received for betraying Jesus.

Language:

The language used in both passages conveys the tragic nature of Judas' actions and the consequences of his betrayal. Matthew's account emphasizes Judas' remorse and the method of his death, highlighting the fulfillment of Old Testament prophecy regarding the fate of the betrayer. Acts adds further details about the field purchased with the money Judas received, which became known as the Field of Blood.

Historical Background:

Understanding the historical context of Judas' betrayal and subsequent death sheds light on the events described in Matthew 27 and Acts 1. Judas' actions took place within the volatile political and religious climate of first-century Judea, characterized by tensions between Roman authorities and Jewish leaders. The significance of the Field of Blood may reflect local traditions or historical landmarks known to early Christian communities.

Theological Considerations:

The fate of Judas Iscariot carries theological implications regarding divine judgment, human responsibility, and the sovereignty of God. Both passages underscore the consequences of betrayal and the tragic outcome of rejecting Jesus. The Field of Blood serves as a somber reminder of the consequences of sin and the need for repentance and forgiveness.

Insights from Scholars, Theologians, and Apologists <u>Various Interpretations and Perspectives:</u>

1. Literary Analysis: Scholars delve into the literary features of both Matthew's Gospel and the book of Acts to discern the authors' intentions and narrative techniques. They explore the unique emphases of each account and consider how literary genre, audience, and theological themes may shape the portrayal of Judas' fate.

2. Theological Reflection: Theologians reflect on the theological implications of Judas' actions and subsequent demise. They consider concepts such as divine sovereignty, human responsibility, and the tension between God's foreknowledge and human free will. Some theologians emphasize the redemptive significance of Judas' role in fulfilling prophecy and facilitating Christ's sacrificial death.

3. Historical Context: Apologists contextualize the accounts of Judas' fate within the broader historical and cultural milieu of first-century Judea. They explore the sociopolitical dynamics of the time, including the complex interactions between Roman authorities, Jewish leaders, and followers of Jesus. By examining historical sources and archaeological evidence, apologists seek to illuminate the historical veracity of the events described in Matthew 27 and Acts 1.

4. Psychological Analysis: Some scholars offer psychological insights into Judas' motivations and mental state. They explore factors such as greed, disillusionment, and spiritual turmoil that may have influenced Judas' decision to betray Jesus and his subsequent despair. By integrating psychological perspectives with biblical texts, scholars aim to deepen our understanding of Judas' character and actions.

5. Redemptive Themes: The fate of Judas Iscariot prompts reflection on broader redemptive themes within Christian theology. Scholars and theologians consider the theological significance of Judas' role in the narrative

of Christ's passion, death, and resurrection. They explore how Judas' actions contribute to the unfolding drama of salvation history and underscore the profound mystery of divine grace and human agency.

6. Interpretive Diversity: Scholars acknowledge the diversity of interpretations surrounding the accounts of Judas' fate. While some emphasize the literal historicity of the biblical narratives, others approach them as symbolic or allegorical representations of theological truths. By engaging with a range of interpretive perspectives, scholars and theologians enrich our understanding of the complexity and depth of biblical texts.

Insights from Scholars, Theologians, and Apologists:

Scholars, theologians, and apologists provide insights into reconciling the accounts of Judas' fate in Matthew 27 and Acts 1. They consider factors such as literary genre, theological themes, and historical context when interpreting the texts. While there may be differences in details between the accounts, the overarching message of Judas' betrayal and its consequences remains consistent.

Summary and Reflection:

Despite variations in the details of Judas' fate between Matthew 27 and Acts 1, both passages convey the tragic outcome of betrayal and the solemnity of divine judgment. Judas' story serves as a cautionary tale about the dangers of greed, deceit, and spiritual betrayal. Ultimately, the fate of Judas Iscariot highlights the complexity of human choices and the need for repentance, forgiveness, and redemption in the face of sin.

16. Jesus' Trial Before the Council

Scripture References:
- Matthew 26:57-68
- Mark 14:53-65
- Luke 22:66-71
- John 18:12-14, 19-24

<u>Analysis</u>

The supposed contradiction here lies in the details surrounding Jesus' trial before the Jewish Sanhedrin council. Each Gospel account (Matthew 26, Mark 14, Luke 22, and John 18) offers variations, creating questions about the exact sequence of events. Here's a breakdown of some key differences:

Witnesses: The Gospels differ on whether there were false witnesses who testified against Jesus (Matthew 26:59-60, Mark 14:56, but not mentioned in Luke or John).

Timing: Mark and Matthew suggest a nighttime trial, while Luke implies it happened closer to dawn.

Peter's Denial: The timing and location of Peter's denial of Jesus also differ slightly between the Gospels.

These discrepancies have led some to question the accuracy of the accounts.

Context:

Each Gospel provides an account of Jesus' trial before the Jewish council, known as the Sanhedrin. While the overarching events are similar, there are variations in the details presented by each Gospel writer. Matthew, Mark, and Luke offer parallel narratives, often referred to as the Synoptic Gospels, while John provides a distinct perspective.

Language:

The language used in the trial accounts reflects the judicial and religious context of first-century Judaism. Each Gospel writer employs distinct terminology and stylistic elements to convey the events surrounding Jesus' interrogation, accusations, and eventual condemnation by the Sanhedrin.

Historical Background:

Understanding the historical and cultural context of Jewish law and governance during the time of Jesus is essential for interpreting the trial accounts. The Sanhedrin served as the supreme council and judicial authority in Jerusalem, responsible for adjudicating both religious and civil matters. Variations in the trial narratives may be attributed to differences in eyewitness testimony, oral traditions, and the theological emphases of the Gospel writers.

Theological Considerations:

The trial of Jesus before the Sanhedrin holds significant theological implications within Christian doctrine. It highlights themes such as injustice, persecution, and the fulfillment of prophecy. The Gospel writers present Jesus as the innocent and righteous Messiah who willingly submits to unjust condemnation for the sake of humanity's redemption.

Insights from Scholars, Theologians, and Apologists <u>Various Interpretations and Perspectives:</u>

1. Textual Analysis: Scholars delve into the nuances of the original language, textual variants, and literary structures of biblical passages to discern the intended meaning of the text. By comparing different manuscript traditions and employing tools of textual criticism, scholars aim to reconstruct the most accurate version of the biblical text available.

2. Historical Context: The historical background of ancient Israel and the broader Near Eastern context provide essential insights into the cultural, political, and religious milieu in which biblical events occurred. Scholars draw on archaeological discoveries, ancient inscriptions, and extra biblical texts to illuminate the historical backdrop of biblical narratives.

3. Literary Genre: Recognizing the diverse literary genres present in the Bible is crucial for interpreting biblical passages accurately. Scholars differentiate between historical narrative, poetry, prophecy, parable, and apocalyptic literature, among others, each requiring distinct interpretive approaches.

4. Theological Reflection: The theological themes and messages conveyed in biblical texts invite theological reflection and interpretation. Theological scholars explore concepts such as redemption, covenant, salvation, and divine sovereignty, discerning the overarching theological framework within which apparent contradictions may be understood.

5. Harmonization: Some scholars attempt to harmonize apparent contradictions by reconciling differences in details, chronology, or perspectives across biblical passages. Harmonization methods may involve identifying

complementary accounts, recognizing variations in eyewitness testimony, or acknowledging editorial processes in the compilation of biblical texts.

6. Historical-Critical Method: The historical-critical method of biblical interpretation seeks to analyze biblical texts within their historical and cultural contexts while employing critical methodologies to evaluate their authenticity, authorship, and transmission. This approach involves rigorous scholarship and interdisciplinary engagement with fields such as archaeology, linguistics, and ancient history.

7. Faith and Interpretation: The role of faith in biblical interpretation is another aspect explored by theologians and apologists. While scholars engage in critical analysis of biblical texts, believers approach Scripture with a posture of trust and reverence, recognizing it as the inspired Word of God. The interplay between scholarly inquiry and faith commitments enriches the interpretive process and fosters deeper spiritual understanding.

8. Theological Diversity: Recognizing the diversity of theological perspectives within the biblical canon allows for a multifaceted interpretation of Scripture. Different authors, communities, and theological traditions contribute to the richness of biblical revelation, offering complementary insights that enrich our understanding of God's purposes and ways.

9. Continued Exploration: The exploration of biblical texts is an ongoing endeavor that invites continual engagement and dialogue among scholars, theologians, and believers. New discoveries, interpretive insights, and theological reflections contribute to the ongoing conversation about the meaning and significance of the Bible for faith and life.

Here are some additional points to consider:

- All four Gospels agree that Jesus was arrested, underwent some form of trial before the Jewish council, and was condemned.
- The variations might reflect the chaotic nature of the events surrounding Jesus' arrest and trial.
- The emphasis might be on the injustice Jesus faced rather than providing a perfectly chronological account.

Understanding these supposed contradictions requires considering the nature of the Gospels and their purpose. They are not meant to be strict historical records but rather theological accounts that emphasize the significance of Jesus' death and resurrection.

Summary and Reflection:

While variations exist in the trial accounts of Jesus before the Jewish council in Matthew, Mark, Luke, and John, these differences do not necessarily indicate contradiction but rather highlight the diverse perspectives and emphases of the Gospel writers. By engaging with the trial narratives in their literary, historical, and theological contexts, readers gain a deeper understanding of the events surrounding Jesus' passion and the significance of his sacrificial death for Christian faith and theology.

17. Details of Paul's Conversion

Scripture References:
- Acts 9:1-19
- Acts 22:6-21
- Acts 26:12-18

<u>Analysis</u>

The supposed contradiction here lies in the details of Paul's (formerly Saul's) conversion on the road to Damascus, recounted in three separate passages of Acts:

Acts 9:

This is the first and most detailed account. It describes Saul journeying to Damascus to persecute Christians. A light flashes, blinding him, and a voice (identified as Jesus) speaks to him. Saul's companions hear the voice but see no one. They take Saul to Damascus where he regains his sight after three days.

Acts 22:

This passage is a speech by Paul himself, addressing a crowd in Jerusalem. He mentions the blinding light and the voice speaking to him, but doesn't mention his companions hearing the voice.

Acts 26:

This is another speech by Paul, this time before King Agrippa. Here, Paul describes seeing a light and hearing a voice, but some details are omitted compared to Acts 9.

The discrepancies lie in:

<u>Companions hearing the voice</u>: Acts 9 says they heard it, while Acts 22 doesn't mention it.

<u>Level of detail</u>: Acts 9 is the most detailed, while Acts 22 and 26 focus more on the core message of Paul's conversion.

Context:

The Book of Acts provides multiple accounts of the conversion of Saul of Tarsus, who later became known as the apostle Paul. Each account offers unique details and perspectives on the events surrounding Paul's encounter with the risen Christ on the road to Damascus. While Acts 9 presents the initial narrative of Paul's conversion, Acts 22 and Acts 26 provide additional insights from Paul's own retelling of the event to different audiences.

Language:

The language used in the three accounts of Paul's conversion reflects the distinctive purposes and audiences of each passage. Acts 9 provides a straightforward narrative of the events, focusing on the miraculous nature of Paul's encounter with Jesus and his subsequent conversion. Acts 22 and Acts 26 include Paul's own testimony, delivered in Aramaic and Greek respectively, emphasizing his personal experience of encountering Christ and his commission to proclaim the gospel.

Historical Background:

Understanding the historical context of Paul's conversion sheds light on the significance of his encounter with Jesus. Saul of Tarsus was a devout Pharisee who persecuted the early Christian church until his dramatic conversion experience on the road to Damascus. The accounts in Acts reflect the early Christian community's memory of Paul's transformation from a zealous opponent of Christianity to one of its most fervent proponents.

Theological Considerations:

The theological significance of Paul's conversion lies in its demonstration of the transformative power of God's grace and the universality of Christ's saving work. Paul's encounter with Jesus not only led to his personal conversion but also marked the beginning of his mission to proclaim the gospel to both Jews and Gentiles. The accounts of Paul's conversion highlight themes of divine sovereignty, redemption, and the call to discipleship.

Insights from Scholars, Theologians, and Apologists <u>Various Interpretations and Perspectives:</u>

Interpreters approach the differences between the three accounts of Paul's conversion from various perspectives. Some view the variations in details and emphasis as complementary rather than contradictory, reflecting the diverse purposes and audiences of the narratives. Others suggest that the differences may stem from variations in oral tradition, eyewitness testimony, or the author's selective presentation of events for literary or theological reasons.

DOES THE BIBLE EVER CONTRADICT ITSELF?: DEMYSTIFYING 50
SUPPOSED INCONSISTENCIES

1. Historical Context: Scholars emphasize the importance of considering the historical context surrounding biblical events. They delve into archaeological findings, ancient manuscripts, and cultural practices to provide insights into the historical accuracy and reliability of biblical narratives. By examining the social, political, and religious milieu of the ancient Near East, scholars offer valuable context for interpreting biblical passages and understanding the perspectives of the authors and their audiences.

2. Textual Analysis: Theologians and biblical scholars employ textual criticism and linguistic analysis to study the original languages of the Bible and discern variations in manuscripts. By comparing different manuscript traditions and textual variants, they seek to reconstruct the most accurate and reliable readings of biblical texts. Through meticulous study of syntax, vocabulary, and literary devices, scholars uncover layers of meaning and nuance in the biblical text, enriching our understanding of its content and message.

3. Theological Interpretation: Theological perspectives play a crucial role in interpreting apparent contradictions within scripture. Theological scholars explore the overarching themes, motifs, and doctrines present in the Bible, seeking to discern the deeper theological truths conveyed by biblical narratives. They examine how different passages contribute to the overarching narrative of salvation history and reflect key theological concepts such as divine sovereignty, redemption, and covenantal relationships.

4. Harmonization Methods: Apologists and biblical scholars propose harmonization techniques to reconcile apparent contradictions in scripture. These methods include examining the literary genre and purpose of each passage, considering the perspectives and theological emphases of the authors, and exploring alternative interpretations that maintain the integrity of the biblical text. By identifying common themes and overarching narratives, scholars offer plausible explanations for apparent discrepancies while upholding the inspiration and authority of scripture.

5. Literary Analysis: The literary features and narrative structure of biblical texts provide valuable insights into their interpretation. Scholars analyze narrative techniques, such as foreshadowing, irony, and parallelism, to uncover layers of meaning and symbolism within the text. By exploring the literary context of biblical passages and their relationship to broader literary genres

and traditions, scholars illuminate the artistry and complexity of biblical storytelling, enriching our appreciation for the depth and beauty of scripture.

6. Cultural and Contextual Insights: Apologists and biblical scholars draw on insights from ancient Near Eastern culture, history, and literature to elucidate the meaning and significance of biblical passages. By examining parallels and cultural norms from neighboring civilizations, they provide valuable context for understanding biblical customs, rituals, and worldview. Cultural insights enhance our interpretation of biblical narratives and illuminate the profound impact of scripture on ancient Israelite society and the surrounding world.

It's important to consider that these are all accounts within the same book, Acts of the Apostles. While there are variations, they all agree on the core message: Paul, a persecutor of Christians, encountered the risen Jesus on the road to Damascus and was dramatically converted. Here are some additional points to consider:

- The focus might be on the transformative nature of Paul's experience rather than providing a perfectly consistent record of every detail.
- The emphasis is on Paul's calling as an apostle to the Gentiles.

Understanding these supposed contradictions requires recognizing the nature of Acts as a historical narrative but also a theological work highlighting the work of the Holy Spirit in spreading the gospel message.

Summary and Reflection:

The multiple accounts of Paul's conversion in Acts highlight the multifaceted nature of his encounter with Jesus and its significance for the early Christian community. While variations in details and emphasis exist between Acts 9, Acts 22, and Acts 26, they converge in affirming the reality of Paul's transformation and his commission to proclaim the gospel. These accounts invite readers to reflect on the transformative power of God's grace and the call to faithful discipleship exemplified in Paul's life and ministry.

18. Jesus' Entry into Jerusalem

Scripture References:
- Matthew 21:1-11
- Mark 11:1-11
- Luke 19:28-44
- John 12:12-19

Analysis

The supposed contradiction here lies in the details surrounding Jesus' triumphant entry into Jerusalem, described in all four Gospels: Matthew 21, Mark 11, Luke 19, and John 12. Here's a breakdown of some key variations:

Number of Animals:

Matthew and Mark mention Jesus riding on a donkey and a colt, while Luke only mentions the colt. John doesn't specify the number of animals.

Location where Jesus finds the Animals:

Matthew and Mark describe Jesus sending disciples to fetch a donkey and a colt, while Luke portrays the colt being found already tied up.

Crowds' Acclamations:

There are some variations in what the crowds say as Jesus enters Jerusalem.

Context:

Each of the four Gospels provides an account of Jesus' triumphant entry into Jerusalem, which is commonly known as the "Triumphal Entry" or "Palm Sunday." While the narratives share similarities, there are also variations in details and emphasis among the accounts.

Language:

The language used in each Gospel narrative reflects the unique style and perspective of the respective evangelists. While there are common elements, such as Jesus riding on a donkey and the crowds shouting "Hosanna," each Gospel writer presents the event with distinct nuances and details.

Historical Background:

Understanding the historical and cultural context of Jerusalem during the time of Jesus is essential for interpreting the Triumphal Entry narratives. The Gospels depict a city filled with anticipation as pilgrims gathered for the Passover festival, a setting ripe for messianic expectations and political tension.

Theological Considerations:

The Triumphal Entry carries significant theological symbolism, particularly in light of Old Testament prophecy and messianic expectations. The use of imagery from Zechariah 9:9, where the coming of the Messiah is foretold, underscores Jesus' identity as the promised King and Savior.

Insights from Scholars, Theologians, and Apologists

<u>Various Interpretations and Perspectives:</u>

1. Literary and Theological Emphases: Scholars note that each Gospel writer has a unique literary and theological agenda, shaping the narrative of the Triumphal Entry to convey specific theological themes. For example, Matthew emphasizes Jesus as the fulfillment of Old Testament prophecy, particularly in his citation of Zechariah 9:9. Mark focuses on Jesus' authority as the Son of God and his confrontations with religious leaders. Luke highlights Jesus' compassion for the marginalized and his concern for Jerusalem's spiritual condition. John emphasizes Jesus' identity as the divine Word made flesh, drawing connections to his role as the Lamb of God.

2. Historical Context: Theological scholars and historians explore the historical and cultural context of Jerusalem during Jesus' time, examining the political, social, and religious dynamics that shaped the events surrounding the Triumphal Entry. They consider factors such as messianic expectations, Roman occupation, and Jewish religious festivals, which provide insights into the significance of Jesus' actions and the reactions of the crowds.

3. Eyewitness Testimony and Oral Tradition: Apologists highlight the role of eyewitness testimony and oral tradition in shaping the Gospel narratives. While the evangelists may have drawn from common sources, including oral traditions and written accounts, variations in details may reflect the diverse perspectives of eyewitnesses and the interpretive choices made by the Gospel writers.

4. Literary Techniques and Symbolism: Theological scholars analyze the literary techniques employed by the Gospel writers to convey theological truths through narrative storytelling. They explore the use of symbolism, imagery, and intertextuality to evoke theological themes and convey the deeper significance of Jesus' actions and words during the Triumphal Entry.

5. Theological Unity Amidst Diversity: Despite the variations among the Gospel accounts, scholars affirm the theological unity of the narratives,

emphasizing the central message of Jesus' identity as the promised Messiah and King. The variations in details do not detract from the overarching theological significance of the event but enrich our understanding of Jesus' multifaceted ministry and mission.

6. Harmonization and Synthesis: Some scholars propose harmonization methods to reconcile the differences among the Gospel accounts, seeking to synthesize the narratives into a cohesive whole while respecting the distinctive emphases of each Gospel writer. This approach involves identifying common elements, reconciling chronological discrepancies, and appreciating the theological diversity present in the Gospels.

Here are some additional points to consider:

- All four Gospels agree that Jesus entered Jerusalem riding on a donkey, which was a sign of humility and fulfilled a prophecy in Zechariah 9:9.
- The variations might reflect the dynamic and celebratory nature of the event with people coming from different directions.
- The emphasis might be on the symbolic nature of the entry rather than providing a perfectly synchronized account of every detail.

Summary and Reflection:

Despite variations in details, the accounts of Jesus' entry into Jerusalem in the four Gospels converge on the central message of Jesus' identity as the promised Messiah and King. The Triumphal Entry serves as a pivotal moment in Jesus' ministry, signaling the culmination of God's redemptive plan and the beginning of the final week leading to the crucifixion and resurrection. As believers reflect on this event, they are reminded of Jesus' sacrificial love, his sovereignty over all creation, and his invitation to join in his kingdom of peace and redemption.

19. The Centurion's Servant

Scripture References:
- Matthew 8:5-13
- Luke 7:1-10

<u>Analysis</u>

The supposed contradiction here lies in the healing of a servant by Jesus, mentioned in both Matthew 8 and Luke 7, but with some variations:

<u>Matthew 8:</u>

A centurion approaches Jesus directly, asking him to heal his servant who is paralyzed and suffering at home. Jesus offers to go and heal him, but the centurion expresses faith that Jesus can heal with just a word. Jesus commends his faith and heals the servant from a distance.

<u>Luke 7:</u>

Elders from the synagogue approach Jesus on behalf of a centurion's "highly valued servant" who is sick and about to die. They speak highly of the centurion and ask Jesus to help. Jesus goes with them to the centurion's house, but before he arrives, messengers from the centurion say the servant has already been healed.

The discrepancies lie in:

- Who approaches Jesus: A centurion himself in Matthew, elders on his behalf in Luke.
- Severity of the illness: Paralyzed in Matthew, sick and about to die in Luke.
- Jesus' movement: Offers to go in Matthew, goes towards the house then heals remotely in Luke.

Context:

In both Matthew 8 and Luke 7, we encounter the story of the Centurion who seeks Jesus' help for his servant who is paralyzed and in great pain. The narratives unfold with the Centurion demonstrating great faith in Jesus' authority to heal his servant. However, there are differences in the context and setting of the encounters between the two accounts.

Language:

While the essence of the conversation between Jesus and the Centurion remains consistent in both Matthew and Luke, there are variations in the wording and phrasing used in the dialogue. These differences may stem from the evangelists' choice of language or the unique perspective each Gospel writer brings to the narrative.

Historical Background:

Understanding the historical context of Roman occupation in Judea provides insights into the dynamics between Jewish society and Roman authorities. The Centurion's status as a Gentile military officer adds layers of complexity to the encounter, highlighting themes of faith transcending social and cultural boundaries.

Theological Considerations:

Both accounts underscore the themes of faith, humility, and divine authority. The Centurion's acknowledgment of Jesus' authority reflects a profound recognition of Jesus' identity as the Son of God. The narratives emphasize Jesus' willingness to respond to genuine faith and his compassion for those in need, irrespective of social status or ethnicity.

Insights from Scholars, Theologians, and Apologists

<u>Various Interpretations and Perspectives:</u>

1. Literary and Theological Emphases: Scholars note that the Gospel writers often emphasize different aspects of Jesus' ministry to convey specific theological messages. In the case of the Centurion's servant, Matthew's Gospel emphasizes Jesus' authority over sickness and disease, highlighting themes of faith and divine healing. Luke, on the other hand, may focus more on the inclusivity of Jesus' ministry and the extension of salvation to all people, including Gentiles. These differing theological emphases may account for variations in details between the two accounts.

2. Historical and Cultural Context: The historical and cultural context of Roman-occupied Judea sheds light on the dynamics of interactions between Jewish society and Roman authorities. The Centurion's status as a Gentile military officer adds layers of complexity to the narrative, reflecting broader themes of faith transcending social and cultural boundaries. Scholars consider the nuances of these cultural dynamics in interpreting the Centurion's encounter with Jesus and its portrayal in the Gospels.

3. Source Criticism and Oral Tradition: Some scholars explore the possibility of different sources or oral traditions underlying Matthew's and Luke's accounts of the Centurion's servant. Variations in details may stem from the use of diverse sources or the evangelists' editorial decisions in shaping their narratives. By examining the literary and redactional processes behind the Gospels, scholars seek to understand the reasons for discrepancies and their theological significance.

4. Theological Reflection: Theological reflections on the Centurion's encounter with Jesus highlight broader themes of faith, healing, and salvation. Jesus' response to the Centurion's faith underscores the universal nature of salvation and the transformative power of genuine belief. The variations between Matthew and Luke invite theological reflection on the diverse ways in which Jesus' ministry impacted individuals and communities, transcending cultural and social barriers.

5. Harmonization and Synthesis: Apologists and theologians employ harmonization techniques to reconcile apparent contradictions between Matthew 8 and Luke 7. They may propose harmonious readings that synthesize details from both accounts while maintaining the central theological message. By considering the complementary nature of the Gospels and their common underlying truths, scholars seek to resolve tensions and illuminate deeper theological insights.

Summary and Reflection:

Despite the differences between Matthew 8 and Luke 7 in the details of the Centurion's encounter with Jesus, both accounts convey the central message of Jesus' authority to heal and his response to genuine faith. The variations in wording and setting add depth to the narrative, underscoring the universal scope of Jesus' mission and the transformative power of faith in him. As readers, we are invited to reflect on the profound implications of this encounter for our own faith journey and our understanding of Jesus' identity and ministry.

20. The Lord's Prayer

Scripture References:
- Matthew 6:9-13
- Luke 11:2-4

<u>Analysis</u>

The Lord's Prayer, though presented in both Matthew 6 (Sermon on the Mount) and Luke 11 (when a disciple asks Jesus to teach them to pray), has some variations, leading to questions about its exact wording.

Here's a breakdown of the differences:

<u>Length:</u>

The prayer in Matthew is longer, including more specific petitions like "daily bread" and "forgive us our debts, as we forgive our debtors."

<u>Wording:</u>

There are some variations in phrasing between the two Gospels (e.g., "Our Father in heaven" vs. "Father").

Context:

In Matthew's Gospel, the Lord's Prayer is part of the Sermon on the Mount, where Jesus delivers teachings on various aspects of discipleship and righteous living. The prayer follows Jesus' instructions on prayer and fasting, emphasizing sincerity, humility, and a focus on God's kingdom. In Luke's Gospel, the Lord's Prayer is introduced in response to a disciple's request to teach them to pray. The context is different, occurring as Jesus is engaged in teaching and ministry.

Language:

While both versions of the Lord's Prayer share common elements, such as addressing God as Father, invoking His kingdom, and seeking provision and forgiveness, they vary in wording and phrasing. Matthew's account is more extensive, including additional petitions and elaborations on forgiveness and deliverance from evil. Luke's version is more concise, focusing on essential aspects of prayer without the same level of detail.

Historical Background:

Understanding the historical and cultural context of Jewish prayer practices sheds light on the composition and transmission of the Lord's Prayer. Jewish prayers often followed specific patterns and included common themes of praise, petition, and thanksgiving. Jesus' teaching on prayer would have resonated with his Jewish audience, drawing on familiar language and concepts.

Theological Considerations:

The theological significance of the Lord's Prayer lies in its role as a model for Christian prayer and a reflection of foundational Christian beliefs. Both Matthew and Luke present Jesus as the authoritative teacher of prayer, emphasizing the centrality of God's kingdom, dependence on God for daily needs, and the importance of forgiveness and spiritual protection.

Insights from Scholars, Theologians, and Apologists

<u>Various Interpretations and Perspectives:</u>

1. Historical and Literary Analysis: Scholars examine the historical context and literary structure of Matthew's and Luke's Gospels to understand their unique theological emphases and audiences. Matthew, writing primarily for a Jewish audience, may have included additional Jewish elements in the prayer, such as the emphasis on God's kingdom and the request for daily bread. Luke, writing for a broader audience, may have presented a more concise version of the prayer to focus on essential themes accessible to all readers.

2. Theological Interpretation: Theological scholars delve into the theological significance of the Lord's Prayer in both Matthew and Luke. They emphasize that while the wording may vary between the two accounts, the essential theological themes remain consistent. These themes include the acknowledgment of God as Father, the request for His kingdom to come, the petition for daily provision, the plea for forgiveness, and the desire for deliverance from evil. These theological truths transcend any differences in wording and highlight the universal nature of Christian prayer.

3. Redactional and Source Criticism: Scholars explore redactional and source-critical theories to explain the variations in the Lord's Prayer between Matthew and Luke. They consider whether the differences arise from the evangelists' editorial decisions, their use of oral tradition or written sources, or theological considerations. Some propose that both Matthew and Luke may have adapted Jesus' teachings on prayer to suit their respective theological and literary agendas while remaining faithful to the core message.

4. Theological Diversity within Unity: Theological diversity within unity is a principle often applied to reconcile apparent contradictions in biblical texts. Scholars highlight that while Matthew and Luke may present different

versions of the Lord's Prayer, these variations reflect the richness and diversity of Jesus' teachings rather than contradictory accounts. Each Gospel writer may have emphasized different aspects of Jesus' prayer, allowing for a multifaceted understanding of prayer's significance in the Christian life.

5. Practical Application: Theological scholars also consider the practical implications of the variations in the Lord's Prayer for Christian worship and discipleship. They emphasize that both versions serve as models for prayer and offer valuable insights into the believer's relationship with God. Christians are encouraged to engage with the Lord's Prayer as a guide for personal and communal prayer, recognizing its enduring relevance and transformative power in their lives.

Here are some additional points to consider:

- Both Gospels agree on the essence of the prayer – a way to connect with God and express core needs and desires.
- The variations might reflect the flexibility of prayer, allowing for personal expression alongside a core structure.
- The focus might be on the underlying themes of reverence, dependence on God, and forgiveness, not on reciting a specific formula.

Summary and Reflection:

Despite variations in wording and context, the Lord's Prayer in Matthew 6 and Luke 11 reflects the core teachings of Jesus on prayer and discipleship. Understanding the historical, cultural, and theological context of each Gospel account enriches our appreciation of the Lord's Prayer as a timeless model for Christian devotion and spiritual formation. As believers, we are invited to engage with the prayer's themes of trust, dependence, and reconciliation, drawing closer to God and embodying His kingdom values in our lives.

21. Jesus' Ascension

Scripture References:
- Luke 24:50-53
- Acts 1:9-11

<u>Analysis</u>

The supposed contradiction here concerns the details of Jesus' ascension into heaven. Here's a breakdown of the variations between:

<u>Luke 24</u>

This passage describes Jesus leading his disciples out to Bethany, blessing them, and then being "lifted up" (ἀνελήφθη, anelephthē) while they watch. A cloud hides him from their sight.

<u>Acts 1</u>

This account mentions Jesus gathering with the disciples after the resurrection. He gives them instructions and then "while they were watching, he was lifted up (ἤρθη, ērthē), and a cloud took him out of their sight." (Acts 1:9)

The discrepancies lie in:

<u>Location:</u> Bethany in Luke, unspecified location near Jerusalem in Acts.

<u>Verb used for Ascension:</u> Slightly different Greek verbs are used in each passage (anelephthē vs. ērthē).

Context:

In Luke 24, the Gospel concludes with the account of Jesus' ascension from the Mount of Olives. This event occurs immediately after Jesus appears to His disciples in Jerusalem and gives them final instructions regarding the proclamation of the gospel. In Acts 1, the narrative continues with a more detailed description of Jesus' ascension, emphasizing the promise of the Holy Spirit and the disciples' commission to be witnesses in Jerusalem and beyond.

Language:

Both accounts describe Jesus' ascension in similar terms, emphasizing His departure from the disciples and His ascent into heaven. While Luke's Gospel provides a concise summary of the event, Acts offers a more detailed narrative, including the presence of angels and Jesus' promise of the Holy Spirit. The language used in both passages underscores the supernatural nature of Jesus' departure and the disciples' response of worship and awe.

Historical Background:

Understanding the historical context of Jesus' ascension helps illuminate the significance of the event for the early Christian community. The ascension marked the culmination of Jesus' earthly ministry and His exaltation to the right hand of God the Father. It also signaled the beginning of the disciples' mission to proclaim the gospel and establish the church, empowered by the Holy Spirit.

Theological Considerations:

The ascension of Jesus holds profound theological significance for Christian faith and doctrine. It affirms Jesus' identity as the exalted Lord and King who reigns over all creation. It also fulfills Old Testament prophecies regarding the Messiah's enthronement and underscores His victory over sin, death, and the powers of darkness. Additionally, the ascension anticipates Jesus' eventual return in glory to consummate His kingdom and establish everlasting reign.

Insights from Scholars, Theologians, and Apologists

<u>Various Interpretations and Perspectives:</u>

1. Literary Analysis: Scholars examine the distinctive literary styles and theological emphases of Luke's Gospel and the book of Acts. They recognize that Luke's Gospel provides a concise summary of Jesus' ascension as the climactic conclusion of His earthly ministry, while Acts offers a more detailed account, emphasizing the significance of the event for the early church. This literary distinction highlights the complementary nature of the two accounts rather than suggesting contradiction.

2. Theological Significance: Theologians emphasize the theological significance of Jesus' ascension for Christian doctrine and faith. They highlight how the ascension affirms Jesus' identity as the exalted Lord and King who reigns over all creation. Moreover, they emphasize its role in inaugurating the era of the church and empowering believers through the outpouring of the Holy Spirit. The ascension also anticipates Jesus' eventual return in glory to establish His eternal kingdom.

3. Historical Context: Apologists delve into the historical context surrounding Jesus' ascension, considering factors such as the early Christian

community's understanding of eschatology and the exaltation of Jesus. They explore how first-century Jewish and Greco-Roman beliefs shaped the early Christians' understanding of Jesus' departure and enthronement. By considering the cultural and religious milieu of the time, apologists provide insights into the significance of the ascension for early Christian theology.

4. Harmonization Techniques: Some scholars propose harmonization methods to reconcile the differences between Luke's account in his Gospel and the narrative in Acts. They suggest that Luke provides a summary of the ascension in his Gospel, focusing on the essential details, while Acts offers additional details to emphasize the significance of the event for the early church. By harmonizing the accounts, scholars highlight the complementary nature of the two narratives.

5. Interpretive Perspectives: Theological scholars explore various interpretive perspectives on Jesus' ascension, considering how different theological traditions approach the biblical texts. They examine how interpretations of the ascension have evolved throughout church history and how diverse theological frameworks shape understandings of its significance. By engaging with a range of interpretive perspectives, scholars enrich the dialogue surrounding Jesus' ascension and its theological implications.

Summary and Reflection:

Despite differences in detail between Luke's account in his Gospel and the narrative in Acts, both passages affirm the reality and significance of Jesus' ascension. The ascension marks the culmination of Jesus' earthly ministry, His exaltation to the right hand of God, and the empowerment of His disciples for mission. As believers, we affirm the truth of Jesus' ascension and look forward to His glorious return in fulfillment of His promises.

22. The Naming of Simon Peter

Scripture References:
- Matthew 16:18
- Mark 3:16
- John 1:42

Analysis

The supposed contradiction here revolves around when and how Simon Peter received his name Peter. There are mentions in all three Gospels and some variations:

Matthew 16:17-18

Jesus declares, "Blessed are you, Simon son of Jonah, for flesh and blood has not revealed this to you, but my Father who is in heaven. And I tell you, you are Peter, and on this rock I will build my church, and the gates of hell shall not prevail against it." (NIV)

Here, Jesus gives Simon the name Peter (Petros in Greek, meaning "rock") after he correctly identifies Jesus as the Messiah.

Mark 3:16-17

This passage introduces Simon Peter as one of the twelve disciples Jesus appoints. There's no mention of Jesus giving him the name.

John 1:40-42

Here, Andrew, Simon's brother, meets Jesus first and then tells Simon, "We have found the Messiah" (identified as "Christ" in some translations). (John 1:41) The passage continues, "Jesus looked at him and said, 'You are Simon, son of John. You shall be called Cephas' (which is translated Peter)." (John 1:42)

The variations are:

- Matthew places the naming in the context of Peter's confession of faith, while John describes it as happening earlier upon meeting Jesus.
- Mark doesn't mention the name-giving at all.

Context:

In Matthew 16, Jesus declares to Simon Bar-Jonah, "You are Peter, and on this rock I will build my church." This statement comes during a conversation where Jesus asks His disciples who they believe He is, and Peter responds, "You are the Christ, the Son of the living God."

In Mark 3, Jesus appoints twelve disciples, including Simon, whom He names Peter. This occurs early in Jesus' ministry, as He selects His inner circle of followers to accompany Him in His ministry.

In John 1, Andrew, Simon Peter's brother, introduces Simon to Jesus. Upon meeting him, Jesus says, "You are Simon the son of John; you shall be called Cephas" (which means Peter).

Language:

The names given to Simon in these passages carry significant meaning. In Matthew 16 and John 1, Jesus uses the Aramaic name "Cephas" or "Kepha," which translates to "rock" or "stone." This signifies Peter's future role in the foundation of the church. In Mark 3, the Greek name "Petros" is used, which also means "rock" or "stone."

Historical Background:

Understanding the cultural and linguistic context of these passages sheds light on the significance of the names given to Simon. In Jewish culture, names often carried symbolic meaning and reflected the character or destiny of the individual. By renaming Simon as Peter or Cephas, Jesus signals his future role and identity within the community of believers.

Theological Considerations:

The naming of Simon as Peter holds theological significance in the New Testament. It symbolizes Peter's leadership role among the disciples and his foundational role in the early church. The name change also underscores Jesus' authority to bestow new identities and missions upon His followers.

Insights from Scholars, Theologians, and Apologists

Various Interpretations and Perspectives:

1. Historical and Cultural Context: Scholars delve into the historical and cultural context of Jewish naming practices during the time of Jesus. They highlight the significance of name changes as indicators of a person's new identity, mission, or role within the community. In this case, the renaming of Simon as Peter symbolizes his future leadership and foundational role within the Christian movement.

2. Linguistic Analysis: Theological experts conduct linguistic analyses of the names used for Simon in each Gospel account. They explore the nuances between the Greek name "Petros" (Peter) and the Aramaic name "Cephas," both of which carry similar meanings related to "rock" or "stone." By examining the original languages and etymology of these names, scholars uncover deeper layers of meaning embedded in the text.

3. Theological Significance: Theological scholars emphasize the theological significance of Jesus' renaming of Simon as Peter. They interpret this act as a demonstration of Jesus' authority and foresight regarding Peter's future role as a key leader in the early Christian community. Peter's name change signifies his pivotal role in establishing the church and serving as a rock-like foundation for the faith.

4. Narrative Purpose: Apologists explore the narrative purposes behind the variations in the Gospel accounts regarding Peter's naming. They consider factors such as the intended audience, theological emphases, and literary styles of each Gospel writer. While the core message remains consistent across the accounts, the specific details may vary based on the author's unique perspective and purpose in presenting the life and teachings of Jesus.

5. Symbolism and Typology: Some scholars delve into the symbolic and typological significance of Peter's name change within the broader biblical narrative. They draw parallels between Peter and figures from the Old Testament, such as Abraham or Joshua, who underwent name changes signifying their new roles in God's plan. By situating Peter's naming within this larger narrative framework, theologians illuminate its deeper theological implications.

6. Ecclesiastical Tradition: The insights of theologians are enriched by the contributions of ecclesiastical tradition, which has long grappled with the theological significance of Peter's role in the Christian church. Drawing from sources such as early church fathers, creeds, and councils, theologians engage with the rich tapestry of theological reflection on Peter's leadership and the significance of his name change.

Summary and Reflection:

Despite variations in the accounts of Simon's naming as Peter in Matthew 16, Mark 3, and John 1, the overarching theme of Jesus bestowing a new identity and mission upon Simon remains consistent. The naming signifies

Peter's future role in the foundation of the church and underscores Jesus' authority to appoint leaders and shape the destiny of His followers. Ultimately, these passages highlight the transformative power of encountering Jesus and being called to participate in His redemptive work.

23. The Number of Paul's Companions at Damascus

Scripture References:

- Acts 9:1-19
- Acts 22:4-16
- Acts 26:9-18

<u>Analysis:</u>

The supposed contradiction here concerns the number of companions with Paul (formerly Saul) on the road to Damascus when he encountered the risen Jesus, as described in three separate passages of Acts:

<u>Acts 9:7</u>

"The men who traveled with him stood speechless, hearing the voice but seeing no one." (NIV)

This implies Paul had companions who witnessed the event.

<u>Acts 22:9</u>

"My companions saw the light, but they did not hear the voice of the one who spoke to me." (NIV)

Here, Paul mentions his companions seeing the light but not the risen Jesus.

<u>Acts 26:13</u>

"While I was journeying with all of them..." (NIV) This is followed by a description of the blinding light and the voice of Jesus speaking to Paul.

The discrepancies lie in the details of what Paul's companions experienced: Hearing the voice: Acts 9 suggests they heard the voice, while Acts 22 contradicts this.

Context:

In Acts 9, Luke recounts Saul's encounter with the risen Jesus on the road to Damascus. Saul, a persecutor of the early Christians, is blinded by a light from heaven and hears Jesus speak to him. Jesus instructs Saul to go into the city, where he will be told what he must do. Saul's companions hear the voice but do not see anyone.

In Acts 22, Saul retells his conversion story to a Jewish audience in Jerusalem. He describes seeing a bright light and hearing Jesus' voice on the road to Damascus. His companions see the light but do not understand the voice of Jesus.

In Acts 26, Saul recounts his conversion once again, this time before King Agrippa. He describes the heavenly vision he received on the road to Damascus, including Jesus' instructions to preach to the Gentiles. His companions fall to the ground but do not hear the voice of Jesus.

Language:

The language used in all three accounts emphasizes the supernatural nature of Saul's encounter with Jesus. Terms such as "light from heaven," "voice," and "vision" highlight the miraculous aspect of the event. While Saul and his companions experience the phenomenon differently in each retelling, the core elements of the experience remain consistent.

Historical Background:

The historical background of Saul's conversion includes his role as a persecutor of the early Christians and his subsequent transformation into the apostle Paul, a key figure in the spread of Christianity. The accounts in Acts reflect the broader narrative of the expansion of the Christian movement and the inclusion of Gentiles in the faith.

Theological Considerations:

The conversion of Saul carries significant theological implications for the early Christian community. It underscores the power of divine intervention in changing hearts and lives, as well as the universality of God's grace and salvation. Saul's transformation into Paul symbolizes the radical change that can occur when individuals encounter the living Christ.

Insights from Scholars, Theologians, and Apologists
<u>Various Interpretations and Perspectives:</u>

1. Historical and Contextual Analysis: Scholars delve into the historical and contextual background of Paul's conversion experience. They consider factors such as the intended audience of each narrative and the purpose of the author in recounting the events. Variations in details, such as the number of Paul's companions, may stem from differences in emphasis, literary style, or the specific retelling of the story for different audiences.

2. Textual Criticism: Theological experts conduct textual criticism to examine the manuscripts and textual variants of the passages in Acts 9, Acts 22, and Acts 26. They evaluate the reliability of the textual tradition and consider whether discrepancies in details such as the number of companions may be attributed to scribal errors, editorial revisions, or other factors affecting the transmission of the text.

3. Theological Interpretation: Apologists explore the theological significance of Paul's conversion experience and the details surrounding it. They highlight the overarching message of Paul's encounter with the risen Christ and his transformation from a persecutor of the church to a devoted follower of Jesus. While the precise number of companions may vary in the different accounts, the core theological themes of repentance, faith, and divine intervention remain consistent.

4. Narrative Perspective: Scholars consider the narrative perspective of each account and its implications for understanding the events at Damascus. They explore whether variations in details such as the number of companions reflect the author's perspective, purpose, or selective presentation of the story to convey a particular message or theme.

5. Eyewitness Testimony: The insights of theologians are enriched by considering the possibility of eyewitness testimony in the accounts of Paul's conversion. While discrepancies may exist in peripheral details, theologians emphasize the reliability of the core narrative and the consistency of the broader themes across the different retellings.

6. Literary Analysis: Apologists engage in literary analysis of the Acts passages to discern the narrative techniques and rhetorical strategies employed by the author. They explore whether variations in details such as the number of companions serve rhetorical purposes or contribute to the overall structure and message of the narrative.

Summary and Reflection:

The variations in the accounts of Saul's conversion in Acts 9, Acts 22, and Acts 26 reflect the diversity of perspectives and audiences addressed by the author, Luke. Despite differences in details such as the experiences of Saul's companions, the central message of divine intervention, repentance, and calling remains unchanged. These accounts serve as powerful testimonies to the transformative power of encountering Jesus and the universality of God's grace and salvation.

24. Jesus' Baptism

Scripture References:
- Matthew 3:13-17
- Mark 1:9-11
- Luke 3:21-22
- John 1:29-34

<u>Analysis:</u>

There are some variations in the Gospel accounts of Jesus' baptism by John the Baptist, but these can be seen as complementary details rather than contradictions. Here's a breakdown of the Gospels mentioning the event:

<u>Matthew 3:13-17</u>

Describes Jesus coming from Galilee to the Jordan to be baptized by John. John initially hesitates, but Jesus insists. After the baptism, the heavens open, and the Holy Spirit descends on Jesus like a dove, and a voice from heaven declares Jesus as God's beloved Son.

<u>Mark 1:7-11</u>

Similar to Matthew, Mark describes John preaching and baptizing, with Jesus coming to be baptized. John recognizes Jesus and is astonished, but Jesus asks to fulfill "all righteousness." After the baptism, the Spirit descends on Jesus like a dove, and a voice from heaven proclaims, "You are my beloved Son; with you I am well pleased."

<u>Luke 3:21-22</u>

This passage is briefer. It mentions Jesus being baptized along with others, and the heavens opening as the Holy Spirit descends on him in bodily form like a dove. A voice from heaven says, "You are my beloved Son; with you I am well pleased."

<u>John 1:29-34</u>

Here, John the Baptist identifies Jesus as the "Lamb of God" who takes away the sin of the world. The Holy Spirit descends on Jesus like a dove, and John the Baptist testifies that this is the Son of God.

The possible variations include:

- Details of John's initial reaction: Matthew and Mark mention John's

hesitation, while Luke and John don't.
- Wording of the heavenly voice: Slight variations exist in the wording across the Gospels.

Context:

In Matthew 3, Mark 1, Luke 3, and John 1, the baptism of Jesus by John the Baptist is recorded. Each Gospel provides unique details surrounding the event, including John's testimony, the descent of the Holy Spirit, and the voice from heaven affirming Jesus as the Son of God.

Language:

The language used in all four Gospel accounts emphasizes the significance of Jesus' baptism. Phrases such as "the heavens were opened," "the Holy Spirit descended like a dove," and "a voice came from heaven" underscore the divine nature of the event. Each Gospel writer employs distinct imagery and language to convey the spiritual and theological implications of Jesus' baptism.

Historical Background:

Understanding the historical context of John the Baptist's ministry and the practice of baptism in first-century Judaism provides insights into the significance of Jesus' baptism. Baptism was a common ritual used for repentance and purification, symbolizing the washing away of sins. John's baptism marked a turning point in Jewish religious practice and paved the way for the ministry of Jesus.

Theological Considerations:

The baptism of Jesus holds profound theological significance in Christian theology. It marks the beginning of Jesus' public ministry and serves as a pivotal moment in His identification with humanity and His mission of redemption. The descent of the Holy Spirit and the voice from heaven affirm Jesus' identity as the beloved Son of God, inaugurating His role as the Messiah and Savior.

Insights from Scholars, Theologians, and Apologists <u>Various Interpretations and Perspectives:</u>

1. Historical and Literary Analysis: Scholars delve into the historical and literary contexts of each Gospel account to understand the unique perspectives and theological emphases of the respective authors. They examine factors such

as the intended audience, cultural background, and theological themes present in each Gospel narrative.

2. Theological Significance: Theologians explore the theological significance of Jesus' baptism in the context of His ministry and mission. They emphasize themes such as divine revelation, the inauguration of Jesus' public ministry, and His identification with humanity. Jesus' baptism serves as a pivotal moment in His earthly life, marking the beginning of His salvific mission and affirming His divine identity as the Son of God.

3. Sacramental and Symbolic Interpretations: Apologists consider the sacramental and symbolic dimensions of Jesus' baptism, particularly in relation to Christian theology and practice. They highlight the parallels between baptism and Jesus' own experience, emphasizing the cleansing from sin, the reception of the Holy Spirit, and the affirmation of one's identity as a child of God. Jesus' baptism serves as a model for Christian initiation and spiritual renewal.

4. Interpretive Harmonization: Scholars and theologians employ harmonization methods to reconcile the differences between the Gospel accounts of Jesus' baptism. They explore potential explanations for variations in details and emphasis, such as differences in eyewitness testimony, editorial decisions by the Gospel writers, or the theological purposes of each Gospel narrative. While the details may differ, the central message of Jesus' baptism remains consistent across all four accounts.

5. Literary and Theological Themes: Scholars analyze the literary and theological themes present in each Gospel account of Jesus' baptism. They explore how each Gospel writer emphasizes different aspects of the event, such as the descent of the Holy Spirit, the voice from heaven, or the role of John the Baptist. These variations contribute to a richer and more nuanced understanding of Jesus' baptism and its theological significance.

6. Unity in Diversity: Apologists emphasize the unity in diversity present in the Gospel accounts of Jesus' baptism. While each Gospel provides a unique perspective on the event, they collectively bear witness to the central truths of Jesus' identity, mission, and ministry. The differences in details and emphasis reflect the diversity of eyewitness testimony and the richness of the Gospel message.

Summary and Reflection:

The baptism of Jesus as recorded in Matthew 3, Mark 1, Luke 3, and John 1 represents a foundational event in Christian theology. Despite variations in details and emphasis, the overarching message of Jesus' identification with humanity, His divine commissioning, and His role as the Son of God remains consistent across all four Gospel accounts. The baptism of Jesus serves as a powerful symbol of initiation into His redemptive mission and a foreshadowing of His ultimate sacrifice for the salvation of humanity.

25. The Crucifixion Narrative

Scripture References:
- Matthew 27:32-56
- Mark 15:21-41
- Luke 23:26-49
- John 19:17-37

Analysis:

The crucifixion narrative across the four Gospels (Matthew 27, Mark 15, Luke 23, and John 19) has some variations, leading to questions about the exact sequence of events. Here's a breakdown of some key supposed contradictions:

Timing of Events:

There are slight differences in the timing of events like the offering of wine, the sayings of Jesus on the cross, and the tearing of the temple curtain.

Women at the Cross:

The Gospels mention different women being present at the crucifixion, though Mary, Jesus' mother, is mentioned by all.

Details of the Crucifixion:

There are variations in details like the inscription placed above Jesus' head and the sayings of the criminals crucified with him.

These discrepancies can be seen as complementary details rather than contradictions.

Context:

Each Gospel presents a unique account of the crucifixion of Jesus Christ, detailing various aspects of the event, including the events leading up to it, the circumstances surrounding it, and the aftermath. While there are similarities among the Gospel narratives, there are also differences in the details provided by each Gospel writer.

Language:

The language used in the crucifixion narratives reflects the distinct styles and theological emphases of the Gospel writers. Each writer employs different terminology and imagery to convey the significance of Jesus' sacrificial death on the cross. While the core events of the crucifixion remain consistent across the Gospels, variations in wording and phrasing contribute to a richer and more nuanced portrayal of the event.

Historical Background:

Understanding the historical and cultural context of crucifixion in the Roman world helps to contextualize the Gospel accounts of Jesus' crucifixion. Crucifixion was a brutal form of execution reserved for the most heinous criminals, designed to inflict maximum pain and humiliation. The Gospel writers likely drew upon their knowledge of crucifixion practices and Jewish customs to narrate the events surrounding Jesus' death.

Theological Considerations:

The crucifixion narratives are central to Christian theology, representing the culmination of Jesus' earthly ministry and the fulfillment of God's redemptive plan. The Gospels emphasize various theological themes in their accounts of the crucifixion, including atonement, redemption, and the victory of Christ over sin and death. Each Gospel writer underscores different aspects of these theological truths in their portrayal of Jesus' death on the cross.

Insights from Scholars, Theologians, and Apologists Various Interpretations and Perspectives:

1. Historical Context Analysis:

Scholars delve into the historical context surrounding crucifixion practices in the Roman Empire. They emphasize that while the core elements of Jesus' crucifixion remain consistent across the Gospels, differences in details may reflect variations in eyewitness testimony, the perspectives of different Gospel writers, and the literary conventions of ancient historiography.

2. Literary and Theological Perspectives:

Theological scholars explore the unique literary styles and theological emphases of each Gospel writer. They highlight how Matthew emphasizes Jesus' fulfillment of Old Testament prophecies, Mark emphasizes Jesus' suffering and humanity, Luke emphasizes Jesus' compassion for the marginalized, and John emphasizes Jesus' divine identity and victory over death. These distinct perspectives enrich our understanding of the multifaceted nature of Jesus' crucifixion.

3. Harmonization Techniques:

Apologists propose harmonization methods to reconcile apparent discrepancies in the crucifixion narratives. They suggest that differences in details, such as the timing of certain events or the inclusion of specific details, may reflect the Gospel writers' intentions to emphasize different aspects of Jesus' crucifixion rather than representing contradictions. By comparing and synthesizing the accounts, scholars aim to construct a cohesive and comprehensive understanding of the events leading up to Jesus' death.

4. Theological Significance:

Theological scholars emphasize the theological significance of Jesus' crucifixion for Christian faith. They highlight how the crucifixion represents the ultimate expression of God's love and Jesus' willingness to lay down His life for humanity's redemption. The differences in the crucifixion narratives underscore the richness and depth of the theological truths conveyed by each Gospel writer, inviting readers to contemplate the profound mystery of Jesus' sacrificial death.

5. Historical Reliability:

Some scholars address questions regarding the historical reliability of the crucifixion narratives. They point out that while variations in details exist, the core elements of Jesus' crucifixion, such as His arrest, trial, crucifixion, and burial, are attested to by multiple independent sources, including early Christian writings and non-Christian historical sources. This convergence of evidence supports the overall reliability of the Gospel accounts.

6. Theological Interpretation:

Theological interpreters explore the theological implications of the crucifixion narratives for Christian doctrine and practice. They emphasize how the crucifixion serves as the foundation of Christian faith, providing the means of salvation and reconciliation between humanity and God. Through Jesus' sacrificial death, Christians are invited to participate in the transformative power of God's grace and to embody the values of love, forgiveness, and self-sacrifice in their lives.

Summary and Reflection:

The crucifixion narratives in Matthew, Mark, Luke, and John provide complementary accounts of the central event in Christian theology—the death of Jesus Christ on the cross. While there are differences in the details and emphasis among the Gospels, the core message remains consistent: Jesus willingly laid down His life as a sacrifice for the sins of humanity, demonstrating God's love and redeeming grace. As Christians reflect on the crucifixion narratives, they are invited to contemplate the depth of God's mercy and the profound implications of Jesus' death for their lives and salvation.

26. The Temptation of Jesus

Scripture References:
- Matthew 4:1-11
- Luke 4:1-13

<u>Analysis:</u>

The supposed contradiction here lies in the order of the temptations Jesus faces in the wilderness, as described in Matthew 4 and Luke 4.

<u>Matthew 4</u>

1. Turn stones into bread (appealing to physical hunger).

2. Throw yourself down from the temple (testing God's protection).

3. Worship the devil in exchange for worldly power.

<u>Luke 4</u>

1. Turn stones into bread (appealing to physical hunger).

2. Take Jesus to a very high mountain and show him all the kingdoms of the world (temptation of power).

3. Take Jesus to the pinnacle of the temple (testing God's protection).

The discrepancy is the order of the second and third temptations (worshiping the devil vs. being on the temple pinnacle).

Context:

Both Matthew 4 and Luke 4 recount the temptation of Jesus immediately following His baptism. In both accounts, Jesus is led by the Spirit into the wilderness, where He fasts for forty days and is subsequently tempted by the devil. While the core elements of the temptation remain consistent, there are variations in the order and wording of the temptations between Matthew and Luke.

Language:

The language used in both accounts emphasizes the spiritual significance of Jesus' temptation. The devil's temptations challenge Jesus to exert His divine authority, test His commitment to God's will, and demonstrate His trust in God's provision. While the specific wording of the temptations varies slightly between Matthew and Luke, the overall themes of temptation, resistance, and victory remain consistent.

Historical Background:

Understanding the historical context of Jewish beliefs and practices during the time of Jesus provides insights into the significance of the temptations. The wilderness was often associated with spiritual testing and preparation, reminiscent of Israel's forty years of wandering in the desert. By facing temptation in the wilderness, Jesus recapitulates Israel's experience and emerges victorious as the faithful Son of God.

Theological Considerations:

The temptation of Jesus carries profound theological significance for understanding His identity and mission. It demonstrates Jesus' humanity as He experiences the full range of human temptation, yet remains sinless. It also highlights Jesus' role as the obedient Son who fulfills God's redemptive plan by overcoming temptation and inaugurating God's kingdom on earth.

Insights from Scholars, Theologians, and Apologists

<u>Various Interpretations and Perspectives:</u>

1. Literary and Theological Emphases: Scholars note that while Matthew and Luke both recount the temptation of Jesus, each Gospel writer emphasizes different aspects of the event to suit their theological purposes. Matthew focuses on Jesus as the fulfillment of Israel's history, presenting Him as the obedient Son who overcomes temptation in the wilderness, echoing Israel's testing in the desert. Luke, on the other hand, emphasizes Jesus' identity as the compassionate Savior who identifies with humanity's struggles. These differing emphases may account for variations in the order and wording of the temptations between the two accounts.

2. Sources and Redaction: The use of different sources or redactional techniques by Matthew and Luke could contribute to variations in their accounts of the temptation. Some scholars propose that Matthew and Luke may have drawn from common oral traditions about Jesus' temptation but adapted them according to their respective theological agendas. Redactional considerations, such as the desire to highlight certain themes or teachings, may also explain differences in the presentation of the temptations.

3. Symbolism and Typology: The temptation narratives in Matthew and Luke are rich in symbolism and typology, drawing on Old Testament motifs and themes to convey theological truths about Jesus' identity and mission. For example, the three temptations in the wilderness parallel Israel's testing in the desert and echo themes of obedience, trust, and fidelity to God. Scholars

interpret these parallels and symbols in light of Jesus' role as the new Adam and the faithful Son who inaugurates God's kingdom.

4. Theological Unity: Despite variations in details, scholars emphasize the theological unity and coherence of the temptation narratives in Matthew and Luke. Both accounts affirm Jesus' identity as the sinless Son of God who triumphs over temptation and inaugurates God's kingdom. The differences in wording or order of the temptations do not detract from the overarching message of Jesus' victory and steadfast commitment to God's will.

5. Historical and Cultural Context: Understanding the cultural and religious context of first-century Judaism is essential for interpreting the temptation narratives. The wilderness was a place associated with spiritual testing and preparation, and Jesus' temptation reflects His identification with humanity's struggles and His role as the faithful Redeemer. By resisting temptation, Jesus demonstrates His qualification to serve as humanity's High Priest and Mediator before God.

Summary and Reflection:

Despite variations in details, the temptation narratives in Matthew 4 and Luke 4 converge to present a cohesive portrait of Jesus' victory over temptation and His unwavering commitment to God's will. These accounts invite believers to emulate Jesus' example by resisting temptation and remaining faithful to God amidst life's trials and challenges. Ultimately, the temptation of Jesus serves as a powerful reminder of His identity as the sinless Savior who triumphs over evil and offers redemption to all who trust in Him.

27. The Day of Jesus' Crucifixion

Scripture References:
- Mark 15:25
- John 19:14-15

<u>Analysis:</u>

The supposed contradiction here concerns the day of Jesus' crucifixion. There are two main perspectives based on the Gospels:

Mark 15:25: "It was the third hour when they crucified him."

- John 19:14-15: "Now it was the day of Preparation of the Passover. It was about the sixth hour. He said to the Jews, 'Behold your King!' They cried out, 'Away with him, away with him, crucify him!' Pilate said to them, 'Shall I crucify your King?' The chief priests answered, 'We have no king but Caesar.'"

* Mark 15: Suggests the crucifixion happened on the "day before the Sabbath" (Mark 15:42). This could be interpreted as Friday, as the Sabbath was on Saturday according to Jewish tradition.

* John 19: Mentions "the Preparation Day of the Passover" before the crucifixion (John 19:14). This could be interpreted as Thursday, as the Passover meal was traditionally prepared on the day before.

Context:

Mark 15 and John 19 both describe the events leading up to Jesus' crucifixion, but they appear to differ in their timing of the crucifixion. Mark's Gospel indicates that Jesus was crucified at the third hour, while John's Gospel places the crucifixion at about the sixth hour.

Language:

The discrepancy in timing between Mark and John may stem from differences in the ways the authors counted time or how they chose to record specific events surrounding Jesus' crucifixion. Mark may have used the Jewish system of counting hours, starting from sunrise, while John may have used the Roman system, beginning at midnight.

Historical Background:

Understanding the cultural and historical context of the Passover and the Roman judicial system sheds light on the timing of Jesus' crucifixion. The day of Preparation for the Passover, mentioned in John 19:14, likely refers to the day before the Passover Sabbath, during which preparations for the Sabbath and the upcoming feast would have taken place. This aligns with the broader narrative of Jesus' crucifixion occurring during the Passover festival.

Theological Considerations:

The timing of Jesus' crucifixion holds theological significance in relation to the fulfillment of Old Testament prophecies and the salvific implications of His death. While the discrepancy in timing may raise questions about historical accuracy, it does not detract from the theological truth of Jesus' sacrificial death and its atoning power for humanity's sins.

Insights from Scholars, Theologians, and Apologists <u>Various Interpretations and Perspectives:</u>

1. Historical Context: Scholars emphasize the importance of understanding the historical and cultural context of the Passover festival and the Roman judicial system during the time of Jesus. The day of Preparation mentioned in John 19 likely refers to the day before the Passover Sabbath, which began at sunset. This preparation day would have involved various activities, including the crucifixion of criminals.

2. Textual Analysis: Theologians delve into the nuances of the Greek text and the wording used in Mark 15:25 and John 19:14-15. They explore whether the discrepancy arises from differences in how the Gospel writers counted time or whether it reflects variations in the sources they used or their theological emphases.

3. Theological Interpretation: Apologists offer theological perspectives on the significance of Jesus' crucifixion in relation to Old Testament prophecies and the Passover festival. They emphasize that the theological truths conveyed in both Mark and John remain intact, regardless of any discrepancies in the timing of specific events.

4. Harmonization Techniques: Some scholars propose harmonization methods to reconcile the apparent contradiction. They suggest that Mark may have used the Jewish system of timekeeping, which started at sunrise, while John may have used the Roman system, which began at midnight. Others propose that the timing mentioned in John 19:14 refers to the start of the legal proceedings rather than the actual crucifixion.

5. Literary Analysis: Theological scholars analyze the literary structures and theological themes of Mark and John to understand why each Gospel writer

may have chosen to emphasize certain details or events. They explore whether the differences in timing serve a broader narrative or theological purpose within each Gospel.

6. Historical Accuracy: Apologists address questions regarding the historical accuracy of the Gospel narratives. They emphasize that minor differences in details or chronology do not detract from the overall reliability of the Gospel accounts, which bear witness to the central truth of Jesus' sacrificial death and resurrection.

Summary and Reflection:

Despite the discrepancy in timing between Mark 15 and John 19 regarding Jesus' crucifixion, both accounts affirm the central truth of His sacrificial death and its significance for salvation. The differences in timing may be attributed to variations in timekeeping systems, the authors' choice of details, or the theological emphases of their respective Gospels. Ultimately, both Mark and John bear witness to the profound reality of Jesus' atoning sacrifice, which remains a cornerstone of Christian faith and theology.

28. The Fate of the Rich Young Ruler

Scripture References:
- Matthew 19:16-30
- Mark 10:17-31
- Luke 18:18-30

Analysis:

The supposed contradiction lies in the details surrounding the fate of the rich young ruler who approaches Jesus, as described in all three Synoptic Gospels (Matthew 19:16-22, Mark 10:17-22, and Luke 18:18-23). Here's a breakdown of the variations:

<u>Matthew and Mark:</u>

Both Gospels depict the rich young ruler going away sorrowful after Jesus tells him to sell his possessions and follow him.

<u>Luke:</u>

Luke's account adds a detail where Jesus observes the ruler's sadness and says, "How hard it is for those who have wealth to enter the kingdom of God!" (Luke 18:24)

The main point of difference is whether the rich young ruler literally walks away or not.

Context:

In all three synoptic Gospels, a rich young ruler approaches Jesus seeking guidance on inheriting eternal life. Jesus responds by instructing him to sell his possessions, give to the poor, and follow Him. The young man leaves saddened because he is unwilling to part with his wealth.

Language:

The language used in these passages emphasizes the importance of wealth and its potential to hinder one's commitment to following Jesus. Jesus' response highlights the challenge of prioritizing material possessions over spiritual devotion.

Historical Background:

Understanding the socio-economic context of Jesus' time provides insights into the significance of wealth and social status. In the ancient Near East, wealth was often equated with power, privilege, and social status. Jesus' teachings challenged societal norms by emphasizing the value of spiritual riches over material wealth.

Theological Considerations:

The encounter with the rich young ruler raises theological questions about the nature of discipleship and the relationship between wealth and salvation. Jesus' call to forsake everything and follow Him underscores the radical demands of discipleship and the need for wholehearted commitment to God.

Insights from Scholars, Theologians, and Apologists Various Interpretations and Perspectives:

1. Theological Themes: Scholars delve into the theological themes embedded in Jesus' encounter with the rich young ruler. They highlight the tension between material wealth and spiritual values, as well as the challenge of surrendering everything to follow Christ. The rich young ruler's reluctance to part with his possessions underscores the radical demands of discipleship and the importance of wholehearted devotion to God.

2. Social and Cultural Context: The socio-economic context of Jesus' time provides crucial background for interpreting the encounter with the rich young ruler. Scholars consider the significance of wealth and social status in ancient Jewish society, where material possessions often conferred power and privilege. Jesus' call to forsake wealth and follow Him would have been particularly challenging in a culture that valued material prosperity.

3. Symbolism and Allegory: Some theologians interpret the rich young ruler allegorically, viewing him as a representative figure symbolizing humanity's struggle with idolatry and attachment to worldly goods. Jesus' response to the young man reflects God's invitation to all believers to surrender their lives fully to Him and prioritize the kingdom of heaven above earthly treasures.

4. Salvation and Grace: Apologists emphasize the broader theological context of salvation and grace in interpreting Jesus' interaction with the rich young ruler. While Jesus' call to sell everything may seem daunting, it ultimately points to the necessity of relying on God's grace rather than personal merit for salvation. The rich young ruler's inability to meet Jesus' conditions highlights the universal human need for divine intervention and redemption.

5. Discipleship and Commitment: The encounter with the rich young ruler prompts reflection on the nature of discipleship and the cost of following

Jesus. Scholars explore the implications of Jesus' teachings for contemporary believers, challenging them to examine their priorities and reevaluate their relationship with wealth and possessions. Jesus' call to radical obedience challenges the status quo and calls for a renewed commitment to Christ-centered living.

6. Ethical and Moral Considerations: The story of the rich young ruler raises ethical questions about wealth, stewardship, and social responsibility. Scholars discuss the practical implications of Jesus' teachings for issues such as economic justice, charity, and the equitable distribution of resources. Jesus' challenge to the rich young ruler challenges believers to reflect on their own attitudes towards wealth and their obligations to those in need.

Summary and Reflection:

Despite variations in the Gospel accounts of the rich young ruler's encounter with Jesus, the overarching message remains consistent: true discipleship requires wholehearted devotion and a willingness to prioritize spiritual values over worldly possessions. The fate of the rich young ruler serves as a cautionary tale about the dangers of attachment to material wealth and the cost of following Jesus. Ultimately, these passages challenge believers to examine their priorities and consider the true source of their security and fulfillment.

29. The Location of Jesus' Tomb

Scripture References:
- Matthew 27:57-61
- Mark 15:42-47
- Luke 23:50-56
- John 19:38-42

Analysis

There isn't a major contradiction concerning the location of Jesus' tomb in the Gospels, but there are some variations in detail across Matthew 27, Mark 15, Luke 23, and John 19. Here's a breakdown:

* All four Gospels mention Jesus being buried in a tomb.

* Matthew 27:60 and Luke 23:53 describe it as a new tomb belonging to Joseph of Arimathea.

* Mark 15:46 and John 19:41 mention a tomb hewn out of rock.

These details are not necessarily contradictory. Here's why:

Context:

Each Gospel provides its unique perspective on the events following Jesus' crucifixion, including the details surrounding His burial. While the core narrative remains consistent across the four accounts, variations in specific details, such as the location of the tomb, have led to questions and interpretations.

Language:

The Gospel writers employ different language and terminology to describe the location of Jesus' tomb, reflecting their individual styles and emphases. While Matthew and Mark mention a tomb belonging to Joseph of Arimathea, Luke refers to it as a tomb hewn in the rock. John describes it as a new tomb in a garden, where no one had yet been laid.

Historical Background:

Understanding burial customs and practices in first-century Judea provides context for interpreting the Gospel accounts. Tombs cut into rock formations were common in the region, reflecting Jewish burial traditions. The mention of Joseph of Arimathea, a member of the Sanhedrin, highlights his role in providing a tomb for Jesus, a gesture of honor and respect.

Theological Considerations:

The location of Jesus' tomb holds theological significance, symbolizing the fulfillment of Old Testament prophecies and the assurance of His resurrection. The Gospels emphasize the temporary nature of Jesus' burial, foreshadowing His victorious triumph over death. The specific details surrounding the tomb underscore Jesus' identity as the promised Messiah and the fulfillment of God's redemptive plan.

Insights from Scholars, Theologians, and Apologists Various Interpretations and Perspectives:

1. Literary and Theological Analysis: Many scholars emphasize the theological and literary themes present in the Gospel narratives. They argue that the variations in the details surrounding the location of Jesus' tomb do not detract from the central message of His death and resurrection. Instead, these differences may reflect the individual emphases and purposes of each Gospel writer. For example, Matthew and Mark may have focused on Joseph of Arimathea's role in providing the tomb as a fulfillment of prophecy, while John may have emphasized the symbolism of the garden setting.

2. Historical and Archaeological Insights: Some scholars draw on historical and archaeological research to provide context for understanding burial practices in first-century Judea. They point out that tombs cut into rock formations were common during that time, and the mention of Joseph of Arimathea providing a tomb aligns with known burial customs. Additionally, archaeological discoveries in Jerusalem have uncovered similar tomb structures, lending credibility to the Gospel accounts.

3. Harmonization Methods: Theological scholars and apologists employ harmonization techniques to reconcile the differences between the Gospel narratives. One approach involves considering the possibility of multiple tombs being involved in Jesus' burial. For example, Joseph of Arimathea's tomb, mentioned in Matthew and Mark, could have been adjacent to the garden tomb described by John. This harmonization preserves the core details of the Gospel accounts while accommodating variations in specific details.

4. Theological Significance: The location of Jesus' tomb holds theological significance for Christians, symbolizing the reality of His death and resurrection. Regardless of the specific details, the overarching truth of Jesus' victory over death remains unchanged. The empty tomb serves as a powerful

testament to the central message of Christianity, affirming the hope of eternal life for believers.

5. Unity of Gospel Message: Ultimately, scholars, theologians, and apologists affirm the unity of the Gospel message despite variations in the details of Jesus' burial. They emphasize that the Gospel writers were not concerned with providing precise geographical coordinates but rather with conveying the essential truth of Jesus' sacrificial death and triumphant resurrection. The variations in the accounts serve to enrich our understanding of these events from different perspectives while affirming the core tenets of the Christian faith.

Summary and Reflection:

The supposed contradiction regarding the location of Jesus' tomb reflects the diversity of perspectives and emphases among the Gospel writers. While variations exist in the details provided, the overall coherence and consistency of the Gospel accounts affirm the truth of Jesus' burial and resurrection. Through careful analysis and interpretation, believers can deepen their appreciation for the richness and complexity of the Gospel narratives, which ultimately point to the central truth of Christ's redemptive work.

30. The Details of Paul's Shipwreck

Scripture References:

- Acts 27
- Acts 28

<u>Analysis:</u>

The supposed contradiction here concerns the details of Paul's shipwreck on his journey to Rome, described in Acts 27 and 28. Here's a breakdown of the variations:

<u>Acts 27</u>

This chapter describes a long and harrowing journey with a violent storm, the crew throwing cargo overboard, and the ship eventually breaking apart on an island called Malta. The people on board survive by swimming or clinging to pieces of the wreckage.

<u>Acts 28</u>

This chapter focuses on Paul's actions on the island, being welcomed by the inhabitants, and eventually continuing his journey to Rome.

The possible supposed contradictions lie in:

- Severity of the Storm: While Acts 27 emphasizes the intensity of the storm, Acts 28 doesn't mention the near-death experience in as much detail.
- Focus of the Passages: Acts 27 is a dramatic narrative about the shipwreck itself. Acts 28 shifts the focus to Paul's ministry after reaching land.

Context:

In Acts 27, Luke provides a detailed account of Paul's journey to Rome, including the shipwreck near the island of Malta. The narrative describes the perilous voyage, the warnings given by Paul, and the eventual shipwreck, followed by the miraculous rescue of all onboard.

In Acts 28, Luke continues the narrative, focusing on Paul's arrival in Malta and his interactions with the locals. While Acts 27 provides a chronological account of the shipwreck and its aftermath, Acts 28 offers additional details about Paul's time on the island and his ministry there.

Language:

The language used in both passages conveys the urgency and danger of the situation during the shipwreck. Acts 27 emphasizes the tumultuous conditions at sea and the efforts of the crew and passengers to navigate the storm. Acts 28 shifts the focus to Paul's interactions with the people of Malta and the hospitality shown to him and his companions after the shipwreck.

Historical Background:

Understanding the historical context of ancient maritime travel is crucial for interpreting the details of Paul's shipwreck. Scholars note that shipwrecks were common occurrences in the ancient Mediterranean world due to unpredictable weather patterns and navigational challenges. The account in Acts 27 aligns with historical accounts of sea voyages from that period, providing insight into the dangers faced by travelers.

Theological Considerations:

Both passages highlight the providential care of God in preserving Paul's life and fulfilling His purpose for Paul's ministry. Despite the perilous circumstances of the shipwreck, Paul remains confident in God's faithfulness and continues to proclaim the gospel to those around him. The narratives underscore the theme of divine protection and guidance amidst adversity.

Insights from Scholars, Theologians, and Apologists Various Interpretations and Perspectives:

1. Historical Accuracy: Scholars examine the historical context of ancient maritime travel, including the prevailing weather patterns, navigational techniques, and common hazards faced by travelers in the Mediterranean region during the first century. They highlight the consistency of Luke's account with known historical details and maritime practices of the time, lending credibility to the reliability of the narrative.

2. Geographical Considerations: The geographical details provided in Acts 27 and Acts 28, such as the names of islands, ports, and landmarks, are subject to scrutiny by scholars and historians. Apologists analyze these details in light of archaeological discoveries and geographical studies to assess the accuracy of Luke's descriptions and their alignment with the geography of the eastern Mediterranean.

3. Nautical Expertise: The technical terminology and descriptions of sailing conditions in Acts 27 demonstrate Luke's familiarity with seafaring practices and terminology. Scholars with expertise in ancient navigation and maritime history assess the accuracy of these details and their consistency with contemporary accounts of shipwrecks and sea voyages.

4. Literary Analysis: The narrative structure and thematic elements of Acts 27 and Acts 28 are examined by theologians and literary scholars to discern the overarching purpose of Luke's account. They explore the theological themes of divine providence, Paul's missionary zeal, and the spread of the gospel in the face of adversity, identifying the narrative's theological significance within the broader context of Luke-Acts.

5. Theological Significance: The shipwreck narratives in Acts highlight themes of divine protection, providential care, and the sovereignty of God over human affairs. Theologians reflect on the spiritual lessons gleaned from Paul's experiences at sea, emphasizing the importance of trust in God's faithfulness, resilience in the face of trials, and the power of faith to overcome adversity.

6. Harmonization Methods: Apologists propose harmonization methods to reconcile any apparent discrepancies between Acts 27 and Acts 28, such as variations in the number of passengers, the duration of the voyage, or the sequence of events. These harmonization efforts aim to demonstrate the complementary nature of the two accounts and their collective reliability as historical records.

Summary and Reflection:

The apparent differences in the details of Paul's shipwreck as described in Acts 27 and Acts 28 do not detract from the overall coherence and reliability of the narrative. Instead, they offer complementary perspectives on Paul's journey to Rome and his ministry during and after the shipwreck. Through careful analysis and interpretation, scholars, theologians, and apologists affirm the historical accuracy and theological significance of the accounts, deepening our understanding of Paul's missionary activities and God's providential care in the face of danger.

31. The Circumcision of Timothy

Scripture References:
- Acts 16:1-3
- Galatians 2:3-5

Analysis:

The supposed contradiction here centers on the circumcision of Timothy.

Acts 16:3

This passage describes Paul and Timothy arriving in Derbe and Lystra. Here, we learn that Timothy "had a believing mother, but a Greek father." Paul then decides to have Timothy circumcised "because of the Jews who were in those places."

Galatians 2:3-5

In his letter to the Galatians, Paul argues forcefully against circumcision as a requirement for salvation. He mentions that even Titus, his companion who was Gentile, was not compelled to be circumcised.

This seems contradictory. If Paul was so against circumcision for salvation, why would he have Timothy circumcised?

Context:

In Acts 16, Timothy is introduced as a disciple in Lystra, where Paul found him and decided to take him along on his missionary journey. Timothy's mother was Jewish, but his father was Greek. Knowing that Timothy's Greek heritage might pose a hindrance to their mission among the Jews, Paul circumcised him to ensure greater acceptance and credibility among the Jewish communities they would visit.

In Galatians 2, Paul recounts his visit to Jerusalem and his interaction with the apostles there. He mentions that Titus, another Gentile companion, was not compelled to be circumcised, emphasizing the freedom and equality of Gentile believers in Christ. This narrative seems to contradict the account in Acts 16, where Timothy is circumcised by Paul.

Language:

The language used in Acts 16 and Galatians 2 reflects the cultural and theological nuances surrounding the practice of circumcision in the early Christian community. While circumcision was a significant issue for Jewish identity and religious observance, its necessity for Gentile believers became a point of contention and debate among early Christian communities.

Historical Background:

Understanding the historical and cultural context of the early church helps illuminate the significance of circumcision and its implications for Gentile believers. The Jerusalem Council, as mentioned in Acts 15, deliberated on the issue of circumcision and concluded that Gentile believers were not required to undergo this Jewish rite as a condition of salvation.

Theological Considerations:

The circumcision of Timothy and the discussion of circumcision in Galatians 2 raise theological questions about the relationship between Jewish and Gentile believers in the early church. Paul's actions with Timothy may have been motivated by pragmatic considerations for effective ministry rather than theological necessity. However, his stance on circumcision in Galatians 2 reflects his broader theological convictions regarding the sufficiency of faith in Christ for salvation.

Insights from Scholars, Theologians, and Apologists Various Interpretations and Perspectives:

1. Historical Context: Scholars emphasize the importance of understanding the historical context of first-century Judaism and the early Christian community. The issue of circumcision was a significant point of contention and debate among Jewish and Gentile believers, reflecting broader questions about identity, inclusion, and observance of Jewish law. The Jerusalem Council's decision in Acts 15 provided crucial guidance on the relationship between Jewish and Gentile believers and set a precedent for navigating cultural and religious differences within the early church.

2. Textual Analysis: Theologians delve into the nuances of the texts in Acts 16 and Galatians 2 to discern Paul's intentions and theological rationale regarding circumcision. While Acts 16 depicts Paul circumcising Timothy for the sake of their mission among Jewish communities, Galatians 2 emphasizes Paul's defense of the gospel of grace and the equality of Gentile believers. Scholars examine the specific wording and context of each passage to understand Paul's approach to circumcision in light of his broader theological convictions.

3. Theological Interpretation: Apologists offer theological perspectives on the significance of circumcision in the early Christian community and its implications for understanding salvation and the identity of believers. They explore Paul's teachings on circumcision in his letters, emphasizing the primacy of faith in Christ over adherence to Jewish rituals or laws. The circumcision of Timothy may be viewed as a pragmatic concession to cultural sensitivities rather than a theological requirement for salvation.

4. Pastoral Considerations: Some scholars highlight the pastoral dimension of Paul's actions with Timothy, suggesting that his decision to circumcise him was motivated by pastoral wisdom and a desire to avoid unnecessary barriers to ministry among Jewish audiences. Paul's approach to circumcision reflects his commitment to contextualizing the gospel message while remaining faithful to its core principles of grace and inclusion.

5. Cultural Dynamics: The cultural dynamics surrounding circumcision in the ancient world and the diverse religious backgrounds of early Christian communities inform scholarly interpretations of Paul's actions with Timothy. Understanding the social, religious, and political context of circumcision sheds light on Paul's strategic approach to ministry and his efforts to bridge cultural divides within the early church.

Summary and Reflection:

The apparent contradiction regarding the circumcision of Timothy in Acts 16 and Galatians 2 underscores the nuanced and context-dependent nature of Paul's ministry and theological teachings. While Paul's actions with Timothy may seem at odds with his broader theological stance on circumcision, they reflect the pragmatic realities and pastoral concerns of early Christian mission and community life. Ultimately, these passages invite readers to grapple with questions of cultural adaptation, theological conviction, and the unity of the church amidst diverse backgrounds and beliefs.

32. The Parable of the Talents

Scripture References:
- Matthew 25:14-30
- Luke 19:11-27

<u>Analysis:</u>

The Parable of the Talents (Matthew 25:14-30) and the Parable of the Minas (Luke 19:11-27) are very similar stories, but with some key differences. Here's a breakdown of what might seem contradictory:

<u>Similarities:</u>

- A master entrusts resources (talents in Matthew, minas in Luke) to servants before going on a journey.
- Some servants use the resources wisely and gain more, while others do nothing.
- The master returns, rewards the faithful servants, and punishes the unproductive one.

<u>Differences:</u>

- Number of Servants: Three in Matthew, ten in Luke.
- Amount Entrusted: Talents were a much larger unit of currency than minas.
- Details of the Unproductive Servant: In Matthew, he buries the talent. In Luke, he hides the mina and offers excuses.
- Reward: In Matthew, the faithful servants are entrusted with even more. In Luke, they are given authority over cities.

These variations might not be contradictions but ways to highlight different aspects of the message.

Context:

In both Matthew and Luke, Jesus tells a parable involving the distribution of talents (a form of currency) by a master to his servants before going away on a journey. The parable emphasizes the importance of stewardship, faithfulness, and accountability in the use of resources and opportunities entrusted to individuals by God.

Differences:

While the core elements of the parable are similar in both accounts, there are notable differences in certain details:

1. In Matthew, the parable mentions three servants who receive talents in varying amounts (five, two, and one talent). Each servant invests or uses the talents entrusted to them, except for the third servant, who buries his talent out of fear.

In Luke, the parable involves ten minas (another form of currency) distributed to ten servants. Unlike Matthew's version, there is no mention of different amounts given to each servant. Instead, each servant is given one mina. The parable focuses on a nobleman who rewards faithful servants and punishes a wicked servant upon his return.

2. The context and timing of the parable differ between Matthew and Luke. In Matthew, Jesus tells the parable during the Olivet Discourse, a series of teachings about the end times. In Luke, the parable is set against the backdrop of Jesus' journey to Jerusalem, with Zacchaeus the tax collector playing a prominent role in the narrative.

Theological Themes:

Despite the differences, both versions of the parable convey similar theological themes:

1. Stewardship and Accountability: Both Matthew and Luke emphasize the responsibility of individuals to use their God-given resources and opportunities wisely and faithfully. The parable underscores the expectation of accountability before God for how one invests and utilizes the blessings entrusted to them.

2. Reward and Judgment: The parable illustrates the principle of divine reward for faithful stewardship and the consequences of negligence or disobedience. In both accounts, the master rewards the faithful servants with greater responsibilities and shares in his joy, while the unfaithful servant faces judgment and loss.

Insights from Scholars, Theologians, and Apologists

Various Interpretations and Perspectives:

1. Literary Analysis and Contextual Understanding: Scholars emphasize the importance of examining the literary genres, themes, and theological emphases of the Gospel accounts to grasp the nuances of Jesus' teachings. They recognize that each Gospel writer had a unique audience and purpose in mind, which influenced their selection and presentation of Jesus' teachings. Therefore, understanding the literary and cultural context of Matthew and Luke's Gospel narratives is crucial for interpreting the Parable of the Talents accurately.

2. Theological Reflections: Theological scholars delve into the deeper theological implications of the Parable of the Talents, considering its significance within the broader context of Jesus' teachings on discipleship, kingdom principles, and eschatological themes. They highlight the overarching theological themes of stewardship, accountability, reward, and judgment present in both Matthew and Luke's accounts. These themes underscore the moral and spiritual responsibilities of believers in utilizing their God-given resources and talents for the advancement of God's kingdom.

3. Harmonization and Comparative Analysis: Apologists and biblical scholars often engage in harmonization techniques to reconcile the differences between Matthew and Luke's versions of the Parable of the Talents. They explore possible explanations for variations in details, such as differences in terminology, audience focus, or theological emphasis. By comparing and contrasting the accounts, scholars seek to discern the underlying message and theological truths conveyed by Jesus through the parable.

4. Historical and Cultural Insights: Understanding the historical and cultural context of first-century Judea provides additional insights into the Parable of the Talents. Scholars consider the economic and social dynamics of the time, as well as the significance of currency, trade, and patronage systems in interpreting Jesus' teachings on wealth, stewardship, and accountability.

5. Redactional and Theological Intentions: Some scholars explore the redactional and theological intentions behind Matthew and Luke's inclusion of the Parable of the Talents in their respective Gospel narratives. They consider how each Gospel writer tailored their account to address the needs and concerns of their audience, emphasizing theological themes and practical applications relevant to their communities.

6. Spiritual and Moral Exhortations: The Parable of the Talents serves as a spiritual and moral exhortation for believers to cultivate faithfulness, diligence,

and stewardship in their Christian walk. Scholars and theologians emphasize the timeless relevance of the parable's teachings for contemporary discipleship, encouraging believers to reflect on their use of talents, resources, and opportunities in service to God and others.

Summary and Reflection:

While the Parable of the Talents in Matthew 25 and Luke 19 may present differences in details and contexts, the underlying theological messages remain consistent. Both versions underscore the principles of stewardship, accountability, reward, and judgment, challenging believers to use their God-given resources wisely and faithfully in anticipation of Christ's return. Rather than focusing solely on the apparent discrepancies, readers are encouraged to glean insights from each version of the parable and apply its timeless truths to their lives.

33. The Resurrection of Lazarus

Scripture References:

- John 11:1-44 (The resurrection of Lazarus)
- John 12:1-11 (Jesus' anointing at Bethany)

Analysis:

The supposed contradiction here concerns the impact of Lazarus' resurrection on the people around him, as described in John 11 and John 12.

<u>John 11</u>

This chapter describes Jesus raising Lazarus from the dead in Bethany. The text mentions some people believing in Jesus because of this miracle (John 11:45). However, others go to inform the chief priests and Pharisees, who then plot to kill both Jesus and Lazarus (John 11:47-53).

<u>John 12</u>

Following Lazarus' resurrection, many people come to see Jesus in Bethany (John 12:9). The chief priests then decide to put Lazarus to death as well (John 12:10).

The contradiction seems to be:

- Initial Belief: Some people initially believe in Jesus after Lazarus' resurrection (John 11:45).
- Later Hostility: The chief priests and Pharisees plot to kill both Jesus and Lazarus (John 11:47-53, John 12:10).

Context:

In John 11, we find the account of Jesus raising Lazarus from the dead in the village of Bethany. Lazarus had been dead for four days when Jesus arrived and performed the miraculous resurrection, demonstrating His power over death and solidifying the faith of those who witnessed the miracle.

In John 12, the narrative shifts to six days before the Passover when Jesus returns to Bethany. Here, we encounter another event in the home of Lazarus, Martha, and Mary, where Mary anoints Jesus' feet with costly perfume.

Literary Analysis:

While both passages take place in Bethany and involve members of Lazarus' household, they focus on different events and themes. John 11 emphasizes Jesus' power to conquer death and the faith of those who witnessed the resurrection of Lazarus. In contrast, John 12 highlights Mary's act of extravagant worship and Jesus' impending betrayal and crucifixion.

Historical Background:

Understanding the social and cultural context of first-century Judea helps to illuminate the significance of these events. Bethany was a village near Jerusalem where Jesus had close friends, including Lazarus and his sisters. The anointing of Jesus by Mary with costly perfume was a gesture of honor and devotion, reflecting the cultural customs of the time.

Theological Considerations:

Both passages contribute to the overarching theological themes of Jesus' ministry, emphasizing His identity as the Son of God and the fulfillment of Messianic prophecy. The resurrection of Lazarus serves as a prelude to Jesus' own resurrection and underscores His authority over life and death. Mary's anointing of Jesus foreshadows His sacrificial death and burial, pointing to the atoning significance of His mission.

Harmonization and Interpretation:

To reconcile the apparent contradiction between John 11 and John 12, scholars and theologians emphasize the complementary nature of the two accounts. Rather than viewing them as contradictory, they interpret them as different events that occurred in the same location with overlapping characters. The resurrection of Lazarus and Mary's anointing of Jesus represent distinct but interconnected aspects of Jesus' ministry and mission.

Insights from Scholars, Theologians, and Apologists <u>Various Interpretations and Perspectives:</u>

1. Literary Analysis and Narrative Context: Scholars analyze the literary structure and narrative context of John's Gospel to understand the theological significance of the events described in chapters 11 and 12. They emphasize the thematic continuity between the two passages, despite their different focal points. John 11 emphasizes Jesus' power over death and the implications of His resurrection for believers, while John 12 foreshadows Jesus' impending death and burial through Mary's anointing.

2. Theological Themes and Symbolism: Theologians explore the theological themes and symbolism present in the resurrection of Lazarus and Mary's anointing of Jesus. They interpret Lazarus' resurrection as a sign of Jesus' divine authority and His role as the source of eternal life. Mary's act of anointing Jesus' feet with costly perfume is seen as an expression of deep reverence, foreshadowing Jesus' sacrificial death and burial.

3. Cultural and Historical Context: Apologists consider the cultural and historical context of first-century Judea to understand the significance of Mary's anointing of Jesus. They highlight the cultural customs surrounding acts of honor and devotion, recognizing Mary's gesture as a profound expression of love and worship.

4. Harmonization Techniques: Some scholars propose harmonization methods to reconcile the apparent contradiction between John 11 and 12. They suggest viewing the events as complementary rather than contradictory, emphasizing the interconnectedness of Jesus' ministry and mission. Rather than presenting conflicting accounts, these passages offer different perspectives on key aspects of Jesus' identity and mission.

5. Theological Implications for Faith: Scholars, theologians, and apologists explore the theological implications of Lazarus' resurrection and Mary's anointing of Jesus for Christian faith and discipleship. They highlight the themes of faith, love, and sacrifice present in these passages, inviting believers to reflect on their own response to Jesus' call and ministry.

6. Historical Reliability and Literary Genre: Scholars examine the historical reliability of the Gospel accounts while also considering their literary genre. While the Gospels are historical documents, they also contain elements of theological interpretation and selective storytelling. Understanding the unique literary features of John's Gospel helps to interpret the events recorded in chapters 11 and 12 within their theological and narrative context.

Summary and Reflection:

The supposed contradiction between John 11 and John 12 regarding the resurrection of Lazarus and Mary's anointing of Jesus underscores the complexity and depth of the Gospel narratives. Rather than presenting conflicting accounts, these passages offer complementary insights into Jesus' ministry, mission, and the response of those who encountered Him. Through critical analysis and theological reflection, readers can gain a deeper appreciation for the multifaceted nature of the Gospel accounts and their significance for faith and discipleship.

34. The Announcement of Jesus' Birth to Shepherds

Scripture References:
- Luke 2:8-20
- Matthew 2:1-12

Analysis:

The supposed contradiction here lies in the fact that only two Gospels, Matthew and Luke, describe the events surrounding Jesus' birth, and they mention different people witnessing it.

Luke 2

Focuses on shepherds being visited by angels and told about the birth of Jesus in Bethlehem. They find Mary, Joseph, and the baby in a manger.

Matthew 2

Describes wise men (often called Magi) following a star to Bethlehem, where they find Jesus and present him with gifts.

There's no mention of shepherds in Matthew, and no mention of wise men in Luke.

Context:

In Luke 2, the announcement of Jesus' birth to the shepherds occurs in the context of the nativity narrative. Angels appear to a group of shepherds in the fields near Bethlehem, proclaiming the good news of Jesus' birth and directing them to find the newborn Savior lying in a manger. The shepherds visit Jesus and spread the news of His birth.

In Matthew 2, the visit of the Magi, or wise men, to Jesus occurs after His birth. The Magi, who have seen a star signifying the birth of the King of the Jews, come to Jerusalem seeking the newborn King. King Herod and the religious leaders of Jerusalem learn of the prophecy that the Messiah would be born in Bethlehem and instruct the Magi to go there.

Language:

In Luke 2, the angels announce Jesus' birth to the shepherds with the proclamation, "Glory to God in the highest heaven, and on earth peace among those whom he favors!" (Luke 2:14, NRSV). The language emphasizes the joyous occasion of Jesus' birth and the peace that His coming brings to humanity.

In Matthew 2, the Magi refer to Jesus as the "king of the Jews" and express their desire to worship Him (Matthew 2:2). Their language highlights the recognition of Jesus' royal identity and their reverence for Him as the Messiah.

Historical Background:

The shepherds in Luke's Gospel represent the humble and marginalized members of society, while the Magi in Matthew's Gospel symbolize the Gentile world. The inclusion of these different groups in the narratives reflects the universal significance of Jesus' birth and mission.

Theological Considerations:

The announcement of Jesus' birth to the shepherds in Luke's Gospel emphasizes themes of humility, divine revelation, and the inclusion of the lowly in God's redemptive plan. The visit of the Magi in Matthew's Gospel highlights themes of kingship, Gentile inclusion, and the recognition of Jesus as the promised Messiah.

Insights from Scholars, Theologians, and Apologists <u>Various Interpretations and Perspectives:</u>

1. Literary and Theological Emphasis: Scholars often emphasize the distinct literary and theological emphases of each Gospel writer. Luke, writing to a predominantly Gentile audience, focuses on themes of inclusivity, humility, and the universal nature of salvation. The announcement of Jesus' birth to the shepherds aligns with Luke's broader narrative of Jesus' concern for the marginalized and His ministry to all people, regardless of social status. On the other hand, Matthew, writing to a Jewish audience, emphasizes Jesus' role as the fulfillment of Old Testament prophecies and the long-awaited Messiah. The visit of the Magi underscores Jesus' royal identity and the Gentile recognition of His kingship.

2. Historical and Cultural Context: Understanding the historical and cultural context of first-century Judea sheds light on the narratives of Jesus' birth in Luke and Matthew. The presence of shepherds in Luke's account reflects the pastoral setting of Bethlehem and the humble circumstances surrounding Jesus' birth. In contrast, the visit of the Magi in Matthew's Gospel resonates with the widespread belief in astrology and the expectation of a coming king among Gentile nations. The inclusion of both Jewish shepherds

and Gentile Magi underscores the universal significance of Jesus' birth and mission.

3. Theological Unity in Diversity: Rather than viewing the differences between Luke's and Matthew's accounts as contradictions, scholars often highlight the theological unity underlying the diversity of the Gospel narratives. Both Luke and Matthew affirm the central truths of Jesus' identity as the Son of God, the Savior of humanity, and the fulfillment of Old Testament prophecy. While the details of the narratives may vary, the overarching message of Jesus' birth as a momentous event in salvation history remains consistent across the Gospels.

4. Harmonization and Interpretation: Some scholars propose harmonization methods to reconcile the chronological and narrative details of Jesus' birth in Luke and Matthew. These approaches involve recognizing the complementary nature of the Gospel accounts and interpreting them in light of each other's theological themes and literary structures. By appreciating the distinct perspectives and emphases of each Gospel writer, scholars aim to deepen their understanding of the multifaceted significance of Jesus' birth for believers of all ages and backgrounds.

Summary and Reflection:

Despite differences in emphasis and detail, the accounts of Jesus' birth in Luke 2 and Matthew 2 both testify to the significance of His coming for humanity. They highlight the universal scope of Jesus' mission and the fulfillment of Old Testament prophecies regarding the Messiah. Rather than viewing these accounts as contradictory, they should be understood as complementary aspects of the Gospel narrative, inviting readers to contemplate the multifaceted significance of Jesus' birth for people of all nations and backgrounds.

35. The Number of Wise Men

Scripture Reference:

Matthew 2:1-12

<u>Analysis:</u>

There isn't actually a contradiction here, but rather a missing detail in the Bible. The supposed contradiction lies in people assuming a specific number of wise men based on the gifts mentioned in Matthew's Gospel.

<u>Matthew 2:1-12</u>

Describes wise men (often called Magi) following a star and bringing gifts of gold, frankincense, and myrrh to Jesus. The text doesn't specify how many wise men there were. The assumption of three wise men comes from the three gifts, but this is not explicitly stated in the Bible.

Context:

In Matthew 2, the Gospel recounts the visit of the Magi, or wise men, to Jerusalem in search of the newborn King of the Jews. These wise men, also known as the Three Kings or Three Wise Men in Christian tradition, are traditionally depicted as bringing gifts of gold, frankincense, and myrrh to the infant Jesus. However, the specific number of wise men mentioned in the Gospel of Matthew is not provided.

Language:

The Gospel of Matthew does not specify the exact number of wise men who visited Jesus. It simply refers to them collectively as "wise men from the east" (Matthew 2:1). The term "Magi" traditionally refers to priests or astrologers from the East, likely Persia or Babylon, who were skilled in interpreting celestial signs.

Historical Background:

The presence of the wise men from the East aligns with historical accounts of astrology and the belief in the significance of celestial events during the time of Jesus' birth. The Magi's journey to Jerusalem in search of the newborn King reflects the widespread expectation of a messianic figure among various cultures and religious traditions.

Theological Considerations:

While the Gospel of Matthew does not specify the exact number of wise men, the theological significance of their visit is clear. The arrival of the Magi underscores the universal nature of Jesus' kingship and the recognition of His divinity by Gentile nations. Their worship of Jesus as the newborn King foreshadows the inclusion of Gentiles in God's redemptive plan and the fulfillment of Old Testament prophecies.

Insights from Scholars, Theologians, and Apologists <u>Various Interpretations and Perspectives:</u>

1. Tradition vs. Scripture: Christian tradition commonly depicts the wise men as three in number, based on the three gifts of gold, frankincense, and myrrh mentioned in Matthew 2:11. However, the Gospel itself does not specify the number of wise men, leaving room for interpretation and speculation.

2. Symbolism vs. Historical Accuracy: Some scholars view the number of wise men as symbolic rather than historically accurate. The three gifts are often interpreted symbolically, representing Jesus' roles as King (gold), High Priest (frankincense), and Sacrifice (myrrh). From this perspective, the number of wise men may not be as significant as the theological message conveyed by their visit.

3. Cultural Context: Understanding the cultural context of astrology and the significance of celestial signs in the ancient Near East provides insights into the Magi's journey and their recognition of Jesus as the King of the Jews. Their visit highlights the intersection of different cultural and religious traditions surrounding the birth of Jesus.

Insights from scholars, theologians, and apologists regarding the number of wise men in Matthew 2 provide valuable perspectives on both the historical context and the theological significance of this passage.

4. Historical Context:

Scholars delve into the historical background of astrology, ancient Near Eastern beliefs, and the role of wise men or Magi in Eastern cultures. They explore how these factors may have influenced the Magi's journey to Jerusalem and their recognition of Jesus as the King of the Jews. Understanding the cultural milieu of the time enhances our interpretation of the biblical narrative and sheds light on the Magi's role in the story of Jesus' birth.

5. Symbolism vs. Literal Interpretation:

The absence of a specific number of wise men in the Gospel of Matthew invites interpretation regarding whether the mention of three gifts implies three wise men. Scholars discuss whether the number three is symbolic rather than literal, representing completeness or perfection, as seen in other biblical contexts. This symbolic approach underscores the theological significance of the Magi's visit rather than focusing on numerical accuracy.

6. Theological Significance:

Theological scholars emphasize the universal message conveyed by the Magi's visit. Regardless of their number, the wise men represent the inclusion of Gentile nations in the fulfillment of Old Testament prophecies and the recognition of Jesus as the Savior of all people. Their worship of Jesus as the newborn King foreshadows the spread of the gospel to the ends of the earth and the establishment of a new covenant that transcends ethnic and cultural boundaries.

7. Tradition and Interpretation:

Apologists and theologians explore the development of Christian tradition surrounding the story of the wise men. While tradition commonly depicts three wise men based on the three gifts, scholars highlight the importance of distinguishing between scriptural accounts and later traditions. They encourage a nuanced approach to interpretation that considers both historical context and theological themes.

8. Cultural and Literary Analysis:

Scholars engage in literary and cultural analysis to discern the intended message of the Gospel of Matthew regarding the Magi's visit. They explore how the narrative functions within the broader structure of Matthew's Gospel and its theological themes, such as the fulfillment of Old Testament prophecies and the identity of Jesus as the Messiah. This holistic approach deepens our understanding of the biblical text and its implications for faith and interpretation.

Summary and Reflection:

The supposed contradiction regarding the number of wise men in Matthew 2 invites careful consideration of both historical context and theological significance. While the Gospel of Matthew does not specify the exact number of wise men who visited Jesus, tradition commonly depicts three wise men based on the three gifts they presented. However, scholars emphasize the importance of distinguishing between scriptural accounts and later traditions, encouraging a nuanced approach to interpretation.

Insights from scholars, theologians, and apologists highlight the universal message conveyed by the Magi's visit, regardless of their number. The wise men represent the inclusion of Gentile nations in the fulfillment of Old Testament prophecies and the recognition of Jesus as the Savior of all people. Their worship of Jesus as the newborn King foreshadows the spread of the gospel to the ends of the earth and the establishment of a new covenant that transcends ethnic and cultural boundaries.

While the specific number of wise men may remain uncertain, the theological significance of their visit remains a central theme in Christian theology and interpretation. The story of the wise men serves as a reminder of God's universal plan of salvation and the invitation for all people to worship and recognize Jesus as Lord and Savior. Ultimately, the supposed contradiction regarding the number of wise men invites readers to delve deeper into the richness of Scripture and the profound truths it conveys about the nature of God's redemptive work in the world.

36. The Purchase of the Field of Blood

Scripture References:
- Matthew 27:3-8
- Acts 1:18-19

<u>Analysis:</u>

The supposed contradiction here concerns the way Matthew 27 and Acts 1 describe the purchase of the field of blood, associated with Judas' death.

<u>Matthew 27:3-8</u>

Describes the chief priests using Judas' returned 30 pieces of silver to buy a potter's field as a burial ground for foreigners. Matthew attributes the name "Field of Blood" to what the priests called it "because of the blood of an innocent man."

<u>Acts 1:18-19</u>

Here, Peter explains that Judas bought the field with the money he received, and falling headlong there, his body burst open. The field is then called "Hakeldama," which means "Field of Blood" in Aramaic.

The variations might seem contradictory because:

- Source of Money: In Matthew, the priests buy the field. In Acts, Judas buys it.
- Reason for the Name: In Matthew, the priests name it for Judas' blood (innocent man). In Acts, it's named for Judas' own violent death.

Context:

In Matthew 27, the Gospel records the tragic end of Judas Iscariot, who betrayed Jesus for thirty pieces of silver. Overcome with guilt, Judas returns the money to the chief priests and elders, who refuse to accept it back. Judas then throws the silver into the temple and goes out and hangs himself. The chief priests, unable to put the money into the treasury since it was blood money, use it to buy the Potter's Field as a burial place for foreigners, naming it the Field of Blood due to its association with blood money.

In Acts 1, Luke recounts the aftermath of Judas Iscariot's betrayal and suicide. Peter addresses the assembled disciples, quoting a prophecy from the Psalms regarding Judas' fate and the need to appoint a replacement among the Twelve Apostles. Peter refers to the Field of Blood as the place where Judas met his demise, stating that Judas purchased the field with the reward of his iniquity and fell headlong, leading to his body bursting open and spilling his intestines.

Language:

Both passages use vivid language to describe the fate of Judas Iscariot and the acquisition of the Field of Blood. Matthew emphasizes the religious and legal implications of the blood money used to purchase the field, highlighting the tragic consequences of Judas' betrayal. Luke provides additional details about Judas' demise, using graphic imagery to convey the gruesome nature of his death.

Historical Background:

Understanding the cultural and historical context of Jerusalem during the time of Jesus and the early church helps illuminate the significance of the Field of Blood. The name may have been derived from its association with blood money or from its use as a burial place for foreigners and strangers. The exact location and details surrounding the acquisition of the field may have varied over time, leading to differences in how it was described in the Gospel of Matthew and the Book of Acts.

Theological Considerations:

The narratives surrounding the Field of Blood raise theological questions about the nature of divine justice, human responsibility, and the consequences of sin. Judas' tragic end serves as a sobering reminder of the destructive power of greed, betrayal, and spiritual blindness. The designation of the field as the Field of Blood underscores the connection between Judas' actions and their consequences, highlighting the need for repentance, redemption, and reconciliation.

Insights from Scholars, Theologians, and Apologists <u>Various Interpretations and Perspectives:</u>

1. Historical Context: Scholars delve into the historical backdrop of Jerusalem during the time of Jesus and the early church. They explore

archaeological evidence and ancient documents to understand the cultural practices related to burial customs, land transactions, and the significance of place names. This historical context sheds light on the plausibility of the events described in the biblical narratives and offers insights into the cultural nuances that may inform the differing accounts of the Field of Blood.

2. Literary Analysis: Theological scholars examine the literary characteristics of Matthew's Gospel and the Book of Acts. They analyze the distinct purposes, audiences, and narrative styles of each text, considering how these factors may influence the portrayal of events such as the purchase of the Field of Blood. Differences in language, imagery, and theological emphases are explored to understand how each author crafted their narrative to convey specific messages to their respective audiences.

3. Theological Interpretation: Apologists and theologians delve into the theological implications of the narratives surrounding the Field of Blood. They explore themes of divine justice, human responsibility, and the consequences of sin, drawing parallels to broader theological motifs present throughout Scripture. The tragic fate of Judas Iscariot and the symbolic significance of the Field of Blood are examined within the framework of God's sovereignty and redemptive purposes.

4. Harmonization Techniques: Some scholars propose harmonization methods to reconcile the differences between Matthew 27 and Acts 1 regarding the acquisition of the Field of Blood. This includes considering alternative interpretations of the events, such as the possibility that Judas initially purchased the field with the blood money before his tragic demise, or that the money he returned indirectly facilitated the acquisition of the field. These harmonization efforts aim to maintain the integrity of both biblical accounts while acknowledging the complexities of historical narrative.

5. Symbolic and Typological Analysis: Theological scholars explore the symbolic and typological significance of the Field of Blood within the broader biblical narrative. They consider its association with Judas' betrayal of Jesus and the consequences of his actions, drawing connections to Old Testament themes of covenant, judgment, and redemption. The Field of Blood may be interpreted as a symbol of the human condition, marked by sin and the need for divine intervention and redemption.

6. Practical Application: Apologists and theologians discuss the practical implications of the narratives surrounding the Field of Blood for contemporary believers. They emphasize the importance of grappling with difficult biblical passages and engaging in rigorous study to deepen understanding and strengthen faith. The tragic account of Judas serves as a cautionary tale against the dangers of spiritual complacency, greed, and moral compromise, prompting reflection on one's own commitment to following Christ faithfully.

Summary and Reflection:

The supposed contradiction regarding the purchase of the Field of Blood invites readers to consider the complex interplay of historical, theological, and narrative elements within the biblical text. While differences in details may exist between Matthew's Gospel and the Book of Acts, the broader themes of divine justice, human accountability, and the redemptive power of God's grace remain central to both narratives. Ultimately, the Field of Blood serves as a poignant reminder of the profound consequences of sin and the transformative hope offered through Christ's sacrifice.

37. The Prophecy of Peter's Denial

Scripture References:
- Matthew 26:31-35
- Mark 14:27-31
- Luke 22:31-34
- John 13:36-38

Analysis:

The supposed contradiction here lies in the details surrounding Jesus' prediction of Peter's denial, as described in all four Gospels: Matthew 26, Mark 14, Luke 22, and John 13. The possible contradictions seem to be: The number of Rooster Crows: Matthew and Mark mention "twice," while Luke and John don't. Here's a breakdown of the variations:

- Matthew 26:34: Jesus predicts Peter will deny him three times "before the rooster crows."
- Mark 14:30: Similar to Matthew, Mark mentions the denial happening "before the rooster crows twice."
- Luke 22:34: Jesus predicts Peter will deny him "three times before the rooster crows."
- John 13:38: Here, Jesus says to Peter, "Truly, truly, I say to you, the rooster will not crow until you have denied me three times."

Context:

In each of the Gospel accounts, Jesus predicts Peter's denial shortly before His arrest and subsequent crucifixion. The predictions occur within the context of the Last Supper, where Jesus shares a final meal with His disciples and delivers important teachings about His impending death and resurrection.

Language:

While the precise wording of Jesus' prediction varies slightly in each Gospel, the core message remains consistent: Peter will deny Jesus three times before the rooster crows. The variations in language may reflect differences in the authors' styles or the specific details they chose to include in their narratives.

Historical Background:

Understanding the cultural and historical context of the Last Supper and Peter's denial sheds light on the significance of these events. In the ancient Near Eastern context, roosters were commonly used to mark the passage of time, particularly in the early morning hours. Jesus' prediction of Peter's denial carries weight against the backdrop of the unfolding events leading to His crucifixion.

Theological Considerations:

The predictions of Peter's denial underscore themes of human weakness, faithfulness, and divine foreknowledge. Jesus' foreknowledge of Peter's actions highlights His omniscience and sovereignty, even in the face of impending betrayal and denial. Peter's subsequent denial and eventual restoration serve as powerful demonstrations of God's grace and mercy.

Insights from Scholars, Theologians, and Apologists <u>Various Interpretations and Perspectives:</u>

1. Historical and Literary Analysis: Scholars examine the historical context and literary characteristics of each Gospel to understand the nuances of Jesus' predictions regarding Peter's denial. They consider factors such as the intended audience, theological themes, and the unique perspectives of the Gospel writers. Through careful analysis, scholars seek to discern the underlying message and theological significance of these predictions.

2. Theological Interpretation: The predictions of Peter's denial raise theological questions about human frailty, divine foreknowledge, and the nature of repentance. Theologians explore the theological implications of Jesus' omniscience and sovereignty in predicting future events, as well as Peter's response to his own failure. They highlight themes of grace, redemption, and the transformative power of repentance in Peter's eventual restoration.

3. Comparative Study of Gospel Accounts: Apologists and biblical scholars engage in comparative studies of the Gospel accounts to reconcile apparent discrepancies in the predictions of Peter's denial. They carefully examine the variations in wording, sequence of events, and contextual details to identify common themes and theological emphases. Through these comparative analyses, scholars aim to harmonize the Gospel narratives while respecting the unique perspectives of each writer.

4. Psychological and Ethical Reflection: The predictions of Peter's denial prompt reflection on the psychological and ethical dimensions of human behavior. Psychologists and ethicists explore the factors that may have

influenced Peter's actions, such as fear, pride, and peer pressure. They also consider the ethical implications of Jesus' response to Peter's denial, emphasizing principles of forgiveness, reconciliation, and moral accountability.

5. Spiritual Application and Personal Reflection: Beyond academic analysis, theologians and pastors offer spiritual insights and practical applications drawn from the predictions of Peter's denial. They encourage believers to examine their own faithfulness, vulnerability to temptation, and reliance on God's grace. Through personal reflection and spiritual discernment, individuals can draw lessons from Peter's experience and cultivate deeper intimacy with God.

6. Theological Diversity and Unity: Scholars acknowledge the diversity of theological perspectives within the Christian tradition regarding the predictions of Peter's denial. While interpretations may vary among different theological traditions, scholars affirm the unity of the Gospel message and the foundational truths of Christian faith. They emphasize the importance of interpreting Scripture in its entirety, recognizing the multifaceted nature of biblical revelation and the overarching themes of God's love, grace, and redemption.

Summary and Reflection:

Despite variations in the precise wording and context of Jesus' predictions of Peter's denial in Matthew 26, Mark 14, Luke 22, and John 13, the overarching message remains consistent across the Gospel accounts. These predictions serve as poignant reminders of human weakness and the need for divine grace and redemption. As believers reflect on Peter's denial and eventual restoration, they are encouraged to cultivate humility, dependence on God, and a willingness to turn back to Him in repentance and faith.

38. The Feeding of the Multitudes

Scripture References:
- Matthew 14:13-21
- Mark 6:30-44
- Luke 9:10-17
- John 6:1-14

Analysis:

There are actually two accounts of the feeding of the multitudes in the Gospels, and these might be the source of the supposed contradiction. Here's a breakdown:

<u>Feeding of the 5,000</u>

This event is described in Matthew 14:15-21, Mark 6:34-44, Luke 9:12-17. Jesus uses five loaves and two fish to feed a multitude near the Sea of Galilee. The leftovers fill twelve baskets.

<u>Feeding of the 4,000</u>

This event is only mentioned in John 6:5-13. Jesus uses seven loaves and a few small fish to feed a multitude near the Sea of Galilee. The leftovers fill seven baskets.

Here's how to understand these accounts:

- Two Separate Events: It's most likely that these passages describe two different miracles of Jesus feeding large crowds with a few provisions.
- Similarities: Both involve Jesus using a small amount of food to feed a large crowd, with leftover baskets.
- Variations in Details: The number of people fed, type and amount of food used, and the number of leftover baskets differ slightly.

Context:

In all four Gospel accounts, Jesus feeds a multitude of people who had gathered to hear Him teach. The event takes place in a desolate place near Bethsaida, and the crowd consists of thousands of men, women, and children. Jesus performs the miracle by multiplying a small amount of food to satisfy the hunger of the entire crowd.

Differences in Details:

While the core narrative remains consistent across the Gospels, there are variations in certain details:

- In Matthew, Mark, and Luke, the disciples suggest sending the crowds away to find food, while in John, Jesus initiates the conversation about feeding the multitude.
- John specifically mentions the boy who provides the five barley loaves and two fish, while the other Gospels do not mention this detail.
- Matthew and Mark mention Jesus instructing the people to sit down on the grass, while Luke simply states that they sat down.
- In John's account, Jesus asks Philip where they can buy bread to feed the crowd, testing him, while this detail is not mentioned in the other Gospels.

Harmonization Efforts:

Scholars and theologians have proposed various harmonization efforts to reconcile the differences in the Gospel accounts of the Feeding of the Multitudes. These efforts include understanding the variations as complementary rather than contradictory, recognizing the different emphases and perspectives of the Gospel writers, and viewing the variations as reflective of eyewitness testimony and oral tradition.

Theological Significance:

Despite the variations in details, the overarching theological significance of the Feeding of the Multitudes remains consistent across the Gospels. The miracle serves as a demonstration of Jesus' compassion, power, and provision. It also points to Jesus as the fulfillment of Old Testament prophecies and the Messiah who satisfies the spiritual hunger of humanity.

Insights from Scholars, Theologians, and Apologists <u>Various Interpretations and Perspectives:</u>

1. Historical and Cultural Context: Scholars delve into the historical and cultural context of first-century Palestine to understand the significance of communal meals and hospitality. They highlight how the Feeding of the Multitudes resonated with Jewish expectations of the Messiah as a provider

and shepherd, drawing on Old Testament imagery of God's provision in the wilderness.

2. Literary Analysis: Theological scholars analyze the literary features of each Gospel account, exploring the unique emphases and theological themes presented by Matthew, Mark, Luke, and John. They consider factors such as narrative structure, vocabulary, and theological motifs to discern the intended messages of the Gospel writers.

3. Theological Themes: Apologists and theologians emphasize the theological themes embedded in the Feeding of the Multitudes, including Jesus' identity as the compassionate and powerful Messiah, the fulfillment of Old Testament prophecies, and the inauguration of God's kingdom. They highlight how the miracle points to Jesus as the Bread of Life who satisfies the spiritual hunger of humanity.

4. Eyewitness Testimony and Oral Tradition: Scholars explore the role of eyewitness testimony and oral tradition in shaping the Gospel narratives, recognizing that variations in details may reflect the diverse perspectives of eyewitnesses and the transmission of oral tradition. They suggest that the variations in the Gospel accounts do not undermine the historical reliability of the event but rather attest to the authenticity of the tradition.

5. Harmonization Efforts: Some theologians propose harmonization efforts to reconcile the differences in the Gospel accounts of the Feeding of the Multitudes. They suggest viewing the variations as complementary rather than contradictory, recognizing the different emphases and purposes of each Gospel writer while affirming the core message of Jesus' compassion and provision.

6. Theological Implications: Apologists and theologians highlight the theological implications of the Feeding of the Multitudes for Christian faith and discipleship. They emphasize the invitation to trust in Jesus as the provider of physical and spiritual nourishment, to participate in God's kingdom work of feeding the hungry, and to embody compassion and generosity in imitation of Christ.

Summary and Reflection:

While variations exist in the details of the accounts of the Feeding of the Multitudes in Matthew, Mark, Luke, and John, these differences do not necessarily indicate contradiction. Instead, they reflect the diverse perspectives of the Gospel writers and the richness of the oral tradition from which they drew. The core message of Jesus' compassion, power, and provision remains consistent, inviting believers to trust in His ability to satisfy both physical and spiritual needs.

39. The Details of Jesus' Betrayal

Scripture References:
- Matthew 26:20-25
- Mark 14:17-21
- Luke 22:21-23
- John 13:21-30

<u>Analysis:</u>

The accounts of Jesus' betrayal across the four Gospels (Matthew 26, Mark 14, Luke 22, and John 13) contain some variations, but these aren't necessarily contradictions. Here's a breakdown of the key points and explanations:

Similarities:

- All Gospels agree that Judas betrays Jesus to the authorities.
- Jesus predicts the betrayal beforehand.
- The betrayal leads to Jesus' arrest.

Variations and Explanations:

- Motivation for Judas:
- Matthew doesn't explicitly mention Judas' motive.
- Mark and Luke mention the money (30 pieces of silver).
- John attributes it to Satan's influence.
- This doesn't necessarily contradict; the Gospels might focus on different aspects of Judas' motivation (greed, external influence, or a combination).

Manner of Betrayal:

- Matthew and Mark describe a kiss as the signal for Jesus' arrest.
- Luke doesn't mention a kiss.
- John mentions the exchange but not a kiss.
- The kiss might be a detail or a symbolic gesture; all Gospels agree on

the act of identification.

Presence of Disciples:

- John 18:10 mentions a disciple (often assumed to be Peter) cutting off the ear of the high priest's servant.
- The other Gospels don't mention this.
- This might be a detail John included, not a contradiction of the others' focus on the main events.

Context:

In the Gospels of Matthew, Mark, Luke, and John, the events surrounding Jesus' betrayal are narrated, each providing unique details and perspectives. While the core elements of the betrayal are consistent across the accounts, differences exist in the timing, participants, and specific actions involved.

Details and Timing:

In Matthew 26, Mark 14, and Luke 22, the betrayal of Jesus occurs during the Last Supper, with Judas Iscariot identified as the betrayer. Matthew and Mark specify that Jesus reveals the betrayer after announcing that one of the disciples would betray Him. Luke also describes Jesus indicating that the hand of the betrayer is with Him on the table. However, John's Gospel places the revelation of the betrayer before the institution of the Lord's Supper and presents a more private interaction between Jesus and Judas.

Participants and Dialogue:

The Gospels vary in their portrayal of the participants involved in Jesus' betrayal and the dialogue that takes place. Matthew and Mark mention Jesus' statement that the betrayer's betrayal is imminent and fulfill the Scripture, while Luke records Jesus' pronouncement of woe to the betrayer. John's Gospel provides additional insights into the internal dialogue of Jesus and Judas during the betrayal, including Jesus' indication of the betrayer through the dipping of bread.

Theological and Literary Considerations:

Theological scholars emphasize that the variations in the Gospel accounts of Jesus' betrayal reflect the different theological emphases and narrative purposes of the Gospel writers. Each Gospel writer selects and arranges the material according to their theological objectives and the needs of their audience. The differences in timing, dialogue, and emphasis contribute to the rich tapestry of the Gospel narratives.

Eyewitness Testimony and Oral Tradition:

Apologists and theologians highlight the role of eyewitness testimony and oral tradition in shaping the Gospel accounts of Jesus' betrayal. While variations exist in the details, the core events surrounding Jesus' betrayal remain consistent across the accounts, indicating the reliability of the tradition.

Harmonization Efforts:

Some scholars propose harmonization efforts to reconcile the differences between the Gospel accounts of Jesus' betrayal. They suggest viewing the variations as complementary rather than contradictory, recognizing the diverse perspectives and purposes of the Gospel writers. Harmonization involves integrating the details from each Gospel into a cohesive narrative that respects the integrity of each account.

Insights from Scholars, Theologians, and Apologists Various Interpretations and Perspectives:

1. Literary and Theological Perspectives: Scholars often approach the Gospel narratives as theological and literary compositions rather than strict historical records. They highlight the unique theological emphases of each Gospel writer and how their narrative choices serve their theological purposes. For example, Matthew presents Jesus as the fulfillment of Old Testament prophecy, while Mark emphasizes Jesus' suffering and servanthood. Luke focuses on the universality of salvation, and John emphasizes Jesus' divine identity. Understanding these distinct theological perspectives helps reconcile differences in details, including the portrayal of Jesus' betrayal.

2. Source Criticism and Redactional Analysis: The field of source criticism examines the sources behind the Gospel narratives and how they were compiled and edited by the Gospel writers. Scholars analyze the synoptic problem, which addresses the literary relationship between the Gospels of Matthew, Mark, and Luke, to understand how shared material and unique content were incorporated. Redactional analysis explores how Gospel writers

edited and adapted existing traditions to convey their theological messages. By examining the sources and editorial decisions behind the betrayal narratives, scholars can identify underlying themes and motifs that contribute to the differences between the accounts.

3. Eyewitness Testimony and Oral Tradition: Apologists and theologians affirm the reliability of the Gospel narratives as products of eyewitness testimony and oral tradition passed down within the early Christian communities. While variations exist in the details of Jesus' betrayal, the core events are consistent across the accounts, indicating the trustworthiness of the tradition. Apologists argue that minor differences in details, such as timing and dialogue, are typical of eyewitness testimony and do not undermine the overall historical reliability of the Gospels.

4. Theological Significance of the Betrayal Narrative: The betrayal of Jesus holds profound theological significance in Christian theology, representing themes of human betrayal, divine sovereignty, and redemption. Scholars and theologians interpret the betrayal narratives within the broader theological framework of salvation history, emphasizing Jesus' voluntary sacrifice for the redemption of humanity. They explore how each Gospel writer emphasizes different aspects of the betrayal narrative to convey theological truths about Jesus' identity, mission, and the nature of discipleship.

5. Harmonization and Synthesis: While differences exist between the Gospel accounts of Jesus' betrayal, scholars employ harmonization techniques to reconcile these variations. Harmonization involves integrating the details from each Gospel into a cohesive narrative while respecting the integrity of each account. Some scholars suggest viewing the differences as complementary rather than contradictory, recognizing the diverse perspectives and purposes of the Gospel writers. By synthesizing the Gospel accounts, scholars seek to construct a more comprehensive understanding of Jesus' betrayal and its theological significance.

In summary, insights from scholars, theologians, and apologists provide a multifaceted perspective on reconciling the differences in the Gospel accounts of Jesus' betrayal. By examining the literary, theological, and historical dimensions of the betrayal narratives, scholars offer valuable insights into understanding the complexities of the Gospel accounts and their implications for faith and interpretation.

They emphasize the theological significance of the betrayal narrative, the reliability of the Gospel tradition, and the importance of interpreting the accounts within their historical, cultural, and literary contexts.

Summary and Reflection:

While variations exist in the details of Jesus' betrayal as presented in the Gospels of Matthew, Mark, Luke, and John, the core elements of the narrative remain consistent. These differences provide richness and depth to the Gospel accounts, highlighting the multifaceted nature of the events surrounding Jesus' passion and the diverse perspectives of the Gospel writers. Through careful analysis and interpretation, these variations contribute to a deeper understanding of the significance of Jesus' betrayal in the overall narrative of His ministry and mission.

40. The Details of Jesus' Trial Before Pilate

Scripture References:
- Matthew 27:1-26
- Mark 15:1-15
- Luke 23:1-25
- John 18:28-19:16

<u>Analysis:</u>

The details surrounding Jesus' trial before Pilate present some variations across the Gospels (Matthew 27, Mark 15, Luke 23, John 18-19). These variations might seem contradictory, but they can be understood by considering different perspectives and focuses of each Gospel writer. Here's a breakdown of the key points:

Similarities:

- All Gospels agree that Jesus is brought before Pilate, the Roman governor.
- The accusations against Jesus involve claims of being a king and stirring up trouble.
- Pilate attempts to release Jesus but is pressured by the crowd.
- Jesus is ultimately condemned to crucifixion.

Variations and Explanations:

- Reason for Trial:
- John 18:31 mentions the Jews wanting to avoid the defilement of overseeing an execution during Passover (a concern not mentioned in the Synoptic Gospels).
- This might be an additional detail John included, not necessarily contradicting the others' focus on the political charges.

Pilate's Actions:

- The Gospels portray Pilate as reluctant to condemn Jesus.

- Details of his attempts to avoid execution vary (offering crowd a choice between Jesus and Barabbas - Matthew, Mark, Luke; offering to have Jesus flogged - John).
- These variations might reflect different attempts by Pilate or emphasize his struggle with the decision.

Role of the Crowd:

- All Gospels depict the crowd calling for Jesus' crucifixion.
- Matthew 27:24-25 uniquely describes Pilate washing his hands to absolve himself of responsibility, which the crowd accepts.
- This detail might be symbolic or emphasize the Jewish leaders' role in Jesus' condemnation.

Context:

The four Gospels provide varying details of Jesus' trial before Pontius Pilate, the Roman governor of Judea. While each Gospel writer recounts the events leading up to Jesus' crucifixion, differences exist in the presentation of Pilate's interactions with Jesus, the accusations brought against Jesus, and the outcome of the trial.

Differences in Details:

1. Accusations: Matthew and Mark emphasize the false accusations made against Jesus by the chief priests and elders, focusing on charges related to blasphemy and claims of being a king. Luke presents a more concise account of the accusations, while John emphasizes Jesus' claim to be the Son of God as a central point of contention.

2. Pilate's Interactions: Each Gospel writer portrays Pilate's interactions with Jesus differently. Matthew highlights Pilate's attempt to distance himself from Jesus' fate, including his symbolic gesture of washing his hands. Mark emphasizes Pilate's recognition of Jesus' innocence but acquiescence to the demands of the crowd. Luke portrays Pilate as finding no guilt in Jesus and attempting to release Him, while John emphasizes the dialogue between Pilate and Jesus regarding kingship and truth.

3. Outcome of the Trial: The Gospels differ in their portrayal of the outcome of Jesus' trial before Pilate. Matthew and Mark depict Pilate

succumbing to the pressure of the crowd and handing Jesus over to be crucified. Luke emphasizes Pilate's attempt to release Jesus but ultimately yielding to the crowd's demands. John presents a more nuanced portrayal of Pilate's struggle with Jesus' case, highlighting his repeated attempts to release Him and his eventual capitulation to the Jewish leaders' threats.

Contextual Considerations:

Understanding the socio-political context of first-century Judea is essential for interpreting the trial of Jesus before Pilate. Pilate, as the Roman governor, held significant power but was also sensitive to maintaining order and preventing unrest among the Jewish population. The trial took place against the backdrop of Passover, a volatile time when tensions between the Jewish people and Roman authorities were heightened.

Theological Significance:

The trial of Jesus before Pilate holds profound theological significance in Christian theology, representing themes of innocence, injustice, and the role of human agency in the crucifixion of Jesus. The differing portrayals of Pilate's interactions with Jesus highlight theological themes such as Jesus' innocence, His kingship, and the fulfillment of Old Testament prophecy.

Harmonization Attempts:

Scholars and theologians have proposed various harmonization attempts to reconcile the differences in the Gospel accounts of Jesus' trial before Pilate. Some suggest that each Gospel writer emphasizes different aspects of the trial to convey theological themes or to address the concerns of their respective audiences. Others propose harmonization techniques that integrate details from each Gospel account into a cohesive narrative, recognizing the complementary nature of the Gospels rather than viewing the differences as contradictions.

Insights from Scholars, Theologians, and Apologists Various Interpretations and Perspectives:

1. Historical Context Analysis: Scholars delve into the socio-political climate of first-century Judea to understand the dynamics at play during Jesus' trial before Pilate. They consider Pilate's precarious position as a Roman governor tasked with maintaining order in a volatile region while navigating the religious sensitivities of the Jewish population. This historical context sheds

light on Pilate's decision-making process and the interactions between Roman authority and Jewish religious leaders during Jesus' trial.

2. Literary Criticism and Narrative Analysis: Theological scholars examine the literary techniques employed by the Gospel writers in their accounts of Jesus' trial before Pilate. They explore the differences in narrative style, characterization, and emphasis among the Gospel accounts, considering factors such as audience, purpose, and theological themes. By analyzing the unique perspectives of each Gospel writer, scholars gain insights into the theological significance of Jesus' trial and its implications for the broader narrative of salvation history.

3. Theological Reflections: The trial of Jesus before Pilate holds profound theological significance in Christian theology. Theologians reflect on themes of innocence, injustice, and the role of human agency in the crucifixion of Jesus. They explore theological concepts such as atonement, redemption, and divine sovereignty, considering how Jesus' trial before Pilate fits into the larger narrative of God's plan for salvation. The trial serves as a pivotal moment in Christian theology, highlighting the sacrificial nature of Jesus' death and the fulfillment of Old Testament prophecy.

4. Harmonization Efforts: Apologists and biblical scholars propose harmonization techniques to reconcile the differences among the Gospel accounts of Jesus' trial before Pilate. They seek to integrate the details from each Gospel narrative into a cohesive whole while respecting the distinctive perspectives of the Gospel writers. These harmonization efforts aim to demonstrate the complementary nature of the Gospel accounts and to address perceived discrepancies in a manner consistent with the broader theological themes of the biblical text.

5. Interfaith Dialogue: Scholars engage in dialogue with scholars from other religious traditions, as well as with skeptics and critics, to address questions and objections related to Jesus' trial before Pilate. They seek to foster understanding and promote respectful dialogue by exploring the historical and theological dimensions of the trial within the broader context of religious studies and comparative religion.

Summary and Reflection:

The differences in the Gospel accounts of Jesus' trial before Pilate reflect the diverse perspectives and theological emphases of the Gospel writers. While variations exist in the details of the trial, the overarching narrative portrays Jesus as the innocent Son of God who willingly submits to unjust condemnation for the redemption of humanity. By examining the nuances of each Gospel account, readers can gain a deeper understanding of the theological themes and historical context surrounding Jesus' trial before Pilate.

41. The Sermon on the Mount

Scripture References:
- Matthew 5-7
- Luke 6

Analysis:

The Sermon on the Mount in Matthew 5-7 and the Sermon on the Plain in Luke 6 aren't necessarily contradictions, but present the same teachings in different contexts. Here's a breakdown of the key points:
- Matthew 5-7 (Sermon on the Mount)
- Luke 6 (Sermon on the Plain)
Similarities:

- Both passages contain core teachings of Jesus, emphasizing ethical conduct, compassion, forgiveness, and love for enemies.
- Many teachings overlap, including the Beatitudes, the Golden Rule, and warnings against judgmentalism.

Content:

Matthew's Gospel presents the Sermon on the Mount as a comprehensive discourse where Jesus delivers profound teachings on various aspects of the Christian life, such as humility, righteousness, prayer, and ethical conduct. This sermon is often regarded as a manifesto of the kingdom of God, outlining the attitudes and behaviors expected of Jesus' disciples.

On the other hand, Luke's Gospel records a condensed version of Jesus' teachings, commonly known as the Sermon on the Plain. While it shares some similarities with the Sermon on the Mount, Luke's account emphasizes practical ethics and social justice, reflecting Jesus' concern for the marginalized and oppressed in society.

Language:

Both Matthew and Luke employ vibrant language and vivid imagery to convey Jesus' teachings. Matthew's narrative style often incorporates Old Testament references and Jewish traditions, reflecting his audience's familiarity with Jewish religious practices. In contrast, Luke's Gospel exhibits a more universal tone, emphasizing Jesus' compassion and inclusivity toward all people, regardless of their social status or religious background.

Historical Background:

The historical context of Jesus' ministry in Galilee provides insights into the setting of both sermons. Matthew's Sermon on the Mount likely took place on a hillside, symbolizing Jesus' role as a new Moses delivering divine revelation to His followers. In contrast, Luke's Sermon on the Plain may have occurred on a level place, reflecting Jesus' accessibility and concern for the everyday struggles of ordinary people.

Theological Considerations:

The Sermon on the Mount and the Sermon on the Plain embody key theological themes central to Jesus' ministry. Both sermons emphasize the arrival of the kingdom of God and the transformative power of grace in the lives of believers. They underscore the importance of aligning one's actions with the values of the kingdom, demonstrating love, mercy, and justice in all relationships.

Insights from Scholars, Theologians, and Apologists <u>Various Interpretations and Perspectives:</u>

1. Literary and Redactional Analysis: Scholars analyze the literary structures and redactional features of Matthew and Luke's Gospels to understand the unique presentations of the two sermons. They explore how each Gospel writer shapes the material to fit their theological agendas and the needs of their respective communities. This analysis reveals the theological emphases and thematic differences between the two accounts.

2. Historical Context: Theological scholars delve into the historical context of first-century Galilee to contextualize Jesus' teachings in both sermons. They consider factors such as social dynamics, economic conditions, and religious practices to illuminate the relevance of Jesus' message to his original audience. This historical inquiry helps to bridge the gap between the ancient world and contemporary interpretations of the sermons.

3. Theological Themes: Theological reflections on the Sermon on the Mount and the Sermon on the Plain highlight the central themes of Jesus' teachings, including the kingdom of God, righteousness, mercy, and discipleship. Scholars explore how these themes intersect with broader theological concepts such as salvation, eschatology, and ethics. They emphasize

the radical nature of Jesus' message and its implications for Christian faith and practice.

4. Ethical and Social Implications: Apologists and theologians engage with the ethical and social dimensions of the sermons, drawing connections between Jesus' teachings and contemporary issues such as poverty, injustice, and peacemaking. They challenge believers to embody the values of the kingdom in their personal lives and communities, advocating for social transformation and reconciliation based on Jesus' example.

5. Interpretive Diversity: Scholars acknowledge the diversity of interpretations surrounding the Sermon on the Mount and the Sermon on the Plain within the Christian tradition. They recognize the range of perspectives offered by theologians, pastors, and laypeople throughout history, including allegorical, moralistic, and prophetic readings of the texts. This diversity enriches the ongoing dialogue and reflection on Jesus' teachings.

6. Hermeneutical Approaches: Theological scholars employ various hermeneutical approaches to interpret the sermons, including historical-critical, literary, and theological methods. They explore how different interpretive lenses shape our understanding of the texts and the implications of these approaches for contemporary Christian theology and spirituality.

Summary and Reflection:

While differences exist between Matthew's Sermon on the Mount and Luke's Sermon on the Plain, both passages converge in their portrayal of Jesus as the embodiment of God's kingdom and the exemplar of righteous living. These sermons challenge believers to embody the values of the kingdom in their daily lives, demonstrating love, compassion, and justice to all. As such, they remain foundational teachings for Christians seeking to follow Jesus' example and fulfill His command to love God and love their neighbors as themselves.

42. The Request of James and John's Mother

Scripture References:
- Matthew 20:20-28
- Mark 10:35-45

Analysis:

The supposed contradiction here lies in the details surrounding the request for James and John's high positions in Jesus' kingdom. Let's look at both accounts in Matthew 20:20-28 and Mark 10:35-40:

Matthew 20

Here, Jesus is approached by "the mother of the Zebedee sons" (James and John) who asks if they can sit at Jesus' right and left hand in his glory. Jesus responds by questioning whether they can handle the suffering that comes with following him.

Mark 10

This passage mentions James and John directly approaching Jesus with the request for the places of honor in his kingdom.

Here's how to understand these variations:

- Who Initiates the Request: Matthew describes the mother approaching Jesus, while Mark focuses on James and John themselves.

Content:

Both Matthew 20 and Mark 10 recount a similar incident involving James and John's mother approaching Jesus with a request regarding her sons' positions in His kingdom. She asks Jesus to grant that one of her sons sit at His right hand and the other at His left when He comes into His glory.

Language:

The language used in both passages emphasizes the ambitious request made by James and John's mother. She seeks positions of honor and authority for her sons, highlighting their desire for prominence in Jesus' kingdom. The wording underscores the significance of these positions in the disciples' minds.

Historical Background:

The request reflects the cultural context of first-century Palestine, where positions of honor and status were highly valued. In Jewish society, seating arrangements often symbolized one's rank and influence. The disciples' aspiration for positions at Jesus' right and left hands reflects their understanding of His anticipated Messianic rule.

Theological Considerations:

Jesus' response to the request addresses deeper theological themes related to discipleship, servanthood, and the nature of His kingdom. He contrasts worldly notions of power and authority with the humble, self-sacrificial ethos of His kingdom. Jesus teaches that true greatness comes from serving others rather than seeking positions of prominence.

Insights from Scholars, Theologians, and Apologists <u>Various Interpretations and Perspectives:</u>

1. Historical Contextualization: Scholars delve into the historical context of first-century Jewish society to understand the significance of honor and authority in the disciples' request. They highlight the cultural norms surrounding seating arrangements and the desire for prestige in Jesus' kingdom.

2. Interpretation of Jesus' Response: Theologians offer diverse interpretations of Jesus' response to James and John's mother. Some emphasize Jesus' critique of worldly power dynamics and His redefinition of greatness as service. Others focus on the disciples' misunderstanding of Jesus' Messianic mission and His redirection of their aspirations toward sacrificial love and humility.

3. Theological Implications: Apologists explore the theological implications of Jesus' teaching on servant leadership. They highlight the paradoxical nature of Christian discipleship, which prioritizes humility and selflessness over worldly success and recognition. They emphasize Jesus' example as the ultimate servant leader and call believers to emulate His model in their lives.

4. Application to Contemporary Context: Scholars, theologians, and apologists draw parallels between the disciples' desire for position and status and modern-day struggles with ambition and self-promotion. They challenge

believers to examine their motives and priorities in light of Jesus' teachings on servant leadership and self-sacrificial love.

5. Redemptive Themes: The request of James and John's mother and Jesus' response also evoke redemptive themes of forgiveness, transformation, and the nature of Christ's kingdom. Scholars and theologians explore how Jesus' teachings challenge conventional notions of power and authority and invite believers into a deeper understanding of God's upside-down kingdom.

6. Unity in Diversity: Despite differences in interpretation, scholars, theologians, and apologists affirm the unity of Jesus' teachings across the Gospel accounts. They emphasize the consistency of Jesus' message of humility, servanthood, and sacrificial love, highlighting its enduring relevance for believers of all generations.

Summary and Reflection:

The incident involving James and John's mother challenges readers to reflect on their own ambitions and attitudes toward leadership. Jesus' response underscores the importance of humility, servanthood, and selflessness in His kingdom. As followers of Christ, we are called to emulate His example of sacrificial love and servant leadership, prioritizing the needs of others above our own desires for recognition and status.

43. The Healing of the Blind Man

Scripture References:
- Matthew 20:29-34
- Mark 10:46-52
- Luke 18:35-43

<u>Analysis</u>

The supposed contradiction here concerns the healing of a blind man (or men) near Jericho, described in all three Synoptic Gospels (Matthew 20:29-34, Mark 10:46-52, Luke 18:35-43). Here's a breakdown of the variations:

Similarities:

- All Gospels mention a blind man (or men) being healed by Jesus as he leaves Jericho.

Variations:

- Number of Blind Men:
- Matthew mentions two blind men crying out to Jesus.
- Mark and Luke mention only one blind man.
- This doesn't necessarily contradict the healing itself. Mark and Luke might have focused on one figure for storytelling purposes, while Matthew highlights Jesus healing two.

Location of Healing:

- Luke places the healing as Jesus approaches Jericho.
- Matthew and Mark describe it as Jesus leaving Jericho.
- This discrepancy might be due to:
- Different stages of the journey being emphasized.
- The blind man calling out from afar as Jesus approached.

Context:

In the Synoptic Gospels of Matthew, Mark, and Luke, we encounter the account of Jesus healing a blind man as He passes through Jericho. While the general narrative is consistent across the three accounts, there are variations in the details provided, such as the number of blind men present and the specific sequence of events surrounding the healing.

Matthew's Gospel records Jesus healing two blind men as He leaves Jericho. Mark's Gospel also mentions two blind men, with Bartimaeus being named as the primary recipient of the healing. Luke's account focuses on a single blind man situated at the entrance to Jericho.

Language:

The language used in each Gospel account conveys the urgency and significance of the blind man's encounter with Jesus. Despite variations in the number of blind men mentioned, the narratives emphasize Jesus' compassion, power, and willingness to heal those who call out to Him in faith.

Historical Background:

Understanding the cultural and geographical context of Jericho provides insight into the variations between the Gospel accounts. Jericho was a bustling city with multiple entrances, and it's plausible that different Gospel writers focused on different aspects of the event based on their sources or theological emphases.

Theological Considerations:

The healing of the blind man(s) illustrates Jesus' identity as the Messiah and Son of God, who has the power to restore sight both physically and spiritually. The blind man's cry for mercy reflects the human condition of spiritual blindness and the need for divine intervention for healing and salvation.

Insights from Scholars, Theologians, and Apologists <u>Various Interpretations and Perspectives:</u>

1. Historical Context Analysis: Scholars delve into the historical context surrounding the healing of the blind man(s) to better understand the variations among the Gospel accounts. They explore factors such as Jericho's geographical layout, cultural practices related to begging and healing, and the social dynamics of the time. By examining historical records and archaeological findings, scholars provide valuable insights into the cultural backdrop against which the events unfolded.

2. Literary Analysis and Source Criticism: Theological scholars employ literary analysis techniques to examine the structure, language, and narrative style of each Gospel account. They also apply source criticism methods to

discern potential sources or oral traditions underlying the Gospel narratives. Through meticulous examination of textual details and intertextual connections, scholars uncover nuances that shed light on the distinct perspectives of the Gospel writers and their theological agendas.

3. Theological Interpretation: Theological scholars and apologists offer interpretations of the healing of the blind man(s) that highlight its theological significance within the broader narrative of Jesus' ministry. They explore themes such as divine mercy, compassion, and the restoration of sight as symbols of spiritual enlightenment and salvation. By contextualizing the miracle within the overarching message of Jesus' redemptive mission, theologians elucidate its profound theological implications for believers.

4. Harmonization Attempts: Some scholars and apologists undertake harmonization efforts to reconcile the variations between the Gospel accounts of the healing of the blind man(s). They propose harmonization techniques such as viewing the accounts as complementary rather than contradictory, considering the possibility of multiple blind men being present but one being more prominently featured, or interpreting differences in details as reflective of the authors' selective emphasis rather than factual discrepancies.

5. Theological and Devotional Reflection: The healing of the blind man(s) serves as a rich theological and devotional subject for reflection among scholars, theologians, and apologists. They explore the spiritual significance of blindness and sight, drawing parallels between physical and spiritual sight, and contemplating the transformative power of encountering Jesus' healing touch. Through theological reflection, scholars deepen their understanding of the Gospel narratives and their relevance for Christian faith and practice.

6. Apologetic Considerations: Apologists address potential objections and skepticism regarding the variations in the Gospel accounts of the healing of the blind man(s). They offer reasoned responses to critics, emphasizing the reliability of the Gospel narratives while acknowledging the complexities of historical recording and transmission. Apologists highlight the consistency of the core message across the Gospel accounts and underscore the overarching truth of Jesus' miraculous healing ministry.

Summary and Reflection:

The variations in the accounts of the healing of the blind man(s) demonstrate the complexity of Gospel harmonization and the diverse perspectives of the Gospel writers. Despite the differences, the overarching message of Jesus' compassion, power, and willingness to heal those who call upon Him remains consistent across the Synoptic Gospels. This event serves as a powerful reminder of Jesus' ministry of restoration and the transformative power of encountering Him in faith.

44. The Details of Paul's Conversion as Told by Paul

Scripture References:
   - Acts 9:1-19
   - Galatians 1:11-24

Analysis:

The supposed contradiction here centers on the details of Paul's (formerly Saul's) conversion as described in two places:

Acts 9

This account describes Paul's dramatic conversion on the road to Damascus. He encounters a blinding light, hears Jesus' voice, and regains his sight three days later. Ananias, a disciple, meets Paul and restores his sight.

Galatians 1

In his letter to the Galatians, Paul recounts his conversion experience differently. He emphasizes that he received the gospel directly from Jesus through a revelation and went to Arabia for a time. He mentions meeting Cephas (Peter) in Jerusalem only after three years.

Here's how to understand these variations:

- Acts paints a more detailed picture of the conversion event, including the encounter with Jesus and Ananias.
- Galatians focuses on Paul's independent reception of the gospel from God and his role as an apostle not dependent on the Jerusalem apostles.

Target Audience:

- Acts is a broader narrative about the early church, including Paul's conversion as part of the story.
- Galatians is a letter addressing specific theological concerns, where Paul emphasizes his direct connection to Jesus.

Context:

In Acts 9, Luke records the dramatic conversion of Saul (later known as Paul) on the road to Damascus. The account describes how Saul encountered a blinding light and heard the voice of Jesus, resulting in his conversion to Christianity and subsequent baptism. This narrative is presented as a pivotal moment in the early Christian movement and serves as the catalyst for Paul's ministry.

In Galatians 1, Paul provides autobiographical details about his conversion experience. He emphasizes that his encounter with Jesus was not mediated by human instruction but was a direct revelation from Christ. Paul recounts how, after his conversion, he did not immediately confer with the apostles in Jerusalem but went to Arabia before returning to Damascus.

The account in Acts 9 offers a detailed narrative of Paul's encounter with Jesus on the road to Damascus. It includes the specific details of Saul's vision, his temporary blindness, and his subsequent encounter with Ananias, who restores his sight and baptizes him. Luke's narrative highlights the miraculous nature of Paul's conversion and its immediate impact on his life and ministry.

In contrast, Paul's account in Galatians 1 focuses more on the divine revelation he received directly from Jesus. He emphasizes that his conversion was not based on human teaching or authority but was a result of Christ's personal intervention. Paul also mentions his initial reluctance to engage with the apostles in Jerusalem, choosing instead to spend time in Arabia before returning to Damascus to begin his ministry.

Language:

The language used in both Acts 9 and Galatians 1 emphasizes the divine nature of Paul's conversion experience. Both accounts underscore the supernatural element of Paul encountering Jesus and receiving a direct revelation from Him. While the specific details may vary, the overarching theme of divine intervention remains consistent in both narratives.

Historical Background:

Understanding the historical context of Paul's conversion is essential for reconciling the differences between Acts 9 and Galatians 1. Scholars consider factors such as Paul's Pharisaic background, his zeal for persecuting Christians, and the broader sociopolitical landscape of first-century Judaism and Christianity. By situating Paul's conversion within its historical context, scholars gain insights into the motivations behind Paul's actions and the significance of his transformation for early Christianity.

Theological Considerations:

Theological scholars explore the theological implications of Paul's conversion as presented in Acts 9 and Galatians 1. They examine themes such as divine grace, human agency, and the role of revelation in the Christian faith. Paul's conversion serves as a powerful testament to God's transformative power and His ability to call individuals to faith and ministry despite their past actions or beliefs.

Insights from Scholars, Theologians, and Apologists <u>Various Interpretations and Perspectives:</u>

1. Historical and Cultural Context: Scholars delve into the historical and cultural milieu of the first century, considering factors such as the diverse religious landscape of the Roman Empire, Paul's Pharisaic background, and the emergence of early Christianity. By understanding the sociopolitical and religious dynamics of the time, scholars contextualize Paul's conversion within broader historical developments and movements.

2. Literary Analysis: Theological scholars analyze the literary genres and purposes of Acts and Galatians. They recognize that Acts, written by Luke, serves as a historical narrative of the early Christian movement, while Galatians, authored by Paul, is a letter addressing specific theological concerns. Recognizing the distinct literary conventions and aims of each text helps scholars appreciate the nuanced portrayal of Paul's conversion in Acts 9 and Galatians 1.

3. Theological Significance: Theological reflections on Paul's conversion emphasize its theological significance for Christian doctrine and spirituality. Scholars highlight themes such as divine grace, the sovereignty of God, and the transformative power of encounter with Christ. Paul's conversion serves as a paradigmatic example of God's initiative in calling individuals to faith and ministry and underscores the universal scope of God's redemptive work.

4. Reliability of Sources: Apologists address questions regarding the reliability and historicity of Acts and Galatians as sources for Paul's conversion. They examine factors such as the authorship, date of composition, and intended audience of each text, assessing the extent to which they provide accurate historical information about Paul's life and ministry. Apologists also

consider external corroborating evidence from other ancient sources and archaeological findings to support the credibility of the biblical accounts.

5. Theological Diversity: Scholars acknowledge the theological diversity within the New Testament corpus and the various perspectives presented by different authors. They recognize that Acts and Galatians may emphasize different aspects of Paul's conversion experience to address distinct theological concerns or to serve the purposes of their respective literary genres. Rather than viewing the variations as contradictions, scholars appreciate the richness and complexity of the biblical narrative and the diverse theological insights it offers.

6. Harmonization and Synthesis: Some scholars propose harmonization approaches to reconcile the differences between Acts 9 and Galatians 1 regarding Paul's conversion. This may involve identifying complementary details in the narratives, considering the possibility of chronological or geographical differences, or recognizing the theological emphases of each text. By synthesizing the accounts, scholars aim to present a cohesive understanding of Paul's conversion that honors the integrity of both biblical texts.

Summary and Reflection:

The differences between Acts 9 and Galatians 1 regarding Paul's conversion offer rich opportunities for theological reflection and interpretation. While the accounts may vary in specific details, they converge in affirming the transformative power of God's grace and the central role of Jesus Christ in Paul's life and ministry. Through careful analysis and interpretation, scholars deepen their understanding of Paul's conversion and its enduring significance for the Christian faith.

45. The Sending Out of the Twelve

Scripture References:
- Matthew 10:1-42
- Mark 6:7-13
- Luke 9:1-6

Analysis:

The supposed contradiction here lies in the details surrounding Jesus sending out the twelve disciples (or apostles) on a mission. The three Synoptic Gospels (Matthew 10, Mark 6, Luke 9) describe this event, but with some variations. Let's delve into each account:

<u>Matthew 10</u>

Describes Jesus sending out the twelve apostles specifically to the "lost sheep of the house of Israel." Detailed instructions are given on travel provisions (carry no money bag, extra tunic, or sandals) and how to approach different households.

<u>Mark 6</u>

Mentions Jesus sending out the twelve "two by two." Instructions are given on taking nothing but a staff, wearing sandals, and not having an extra tunic. There's no mention of the mission being limited to the house of Israel.

<u>Luke 9</u>

Jesus sends out the twelve, giving them power and authority over demons and diseases. He instructs them to take nothing for the journey (no staff, bag, bread, or money) and to wear sandals. Similar to Matthew, the focus seems to be on ministering to the Israelites.

Here's how to understand these variations:

- Matthew emphasizes the message for the Israelites and the specific instructions for the disciples.
- Mark focuses on the action of sending them out two by two with minimal provisions.
- Luke highlights the power given to the disciples and the instruction on travel provisions.

DOES THE BIBLE EVER CONTRADICT ITSELF?: DEMYSTIFYING 50 SUPPOSED INCONSISTENCIES

Context:

In all three synoptic Gospels, Jesus sends out His twelve disciples to preach, heal, and cast out demons. While the core message and purpose of the mission are consistent across the accounts, there are variations in the details provided by Matthew, Mark, and Luke.

Matthew 10 provides the most detailed account of the sending out of the twelve disciples. It includes Jesus' specific instructions to the disciples, such as where to go, what to preach, and how to conduct themselves. The chapter also contains teachings on persecution, trust in God, and the cost of discipleship.

Mark 6 and Luke 9 offer more condensed versions of the sending out of the twelve. They highlight Jesus' commissioning of the disciples and their subsequent activities but provide fewer specific instructions compared to Matthew's account.

Language:

The language used in all three accounts emphasizes the authority of Jesus in sending out His disciples and the importance of their mission. Jesus grants them power and authority to heal diseases and cast out demons, underscoring His divine commission and the supernatural nature of their ministry.

Historical Background:

Understanding the historical context of Jesus' ministry and the socio-political environment of first-century Palestine helps contextualize the sending out of the twelve. Jesus' decision to send His disciples on a mission reflects common practices among Jewish teachers of the time, who often sent out their followers to spread their teachings.

Theological Considerations:

The sending out of the twelve carries theological significance, highlighting themes such as discipleship, the kingdom of God, and the authority of Jesus. It demonstrates Jesus' commitment to spreading the message of salvation and extending His ministry through His disciples. The disciples' obedience to Jesus' instructions underscores the importance of faith and trust in God's provision.

Insights from Scholars, Theologians, and Apologists <u>Various Interpretations and Perspectives:</u>

1. Literary Analysis and Theological Themes: Scholars delve into the unique literary styles and theological emphases of each Gospel writer. Matthew, for example, often arranges material thematically, emphasizing Jesus' role as the

new Moses and the fulfillment of Old Testament prophecies. Mark, known for his concise and action-packed narrative, focuses on the authority of Jesus and the urgency of discipleship. Luke, writing with a broader Gentile audience in mind, highlights themes of inclusion, compassion, and the universality of Jesus' message. Understanding these distinct perspectives helps reconcile the differences in the details of the sending out of the twelve.

2. Oral Tradition and Redactional Choices: The variations in the accounts of the sending out of the twelve may also stem from differences in the oral traditions upon which the Gospel writers relied and their redactional choices. Apologists and scholars suggest that while the core message and events remain consistent, minor details may have been shaped by the specific needs and concerns of the communities to which each Gospel was addressed.

3. Historical Context and Cultural Practices: The historical context of first-century Palestine, including the socio-political environment and cultural practices, provides insights into Jesus' ministry and the activities of His disciples. The practice of itinerant preaching and sending out disciples to spread a teacher's message was common among Jewish rabbis of the time. Understanding these cultural norms helps contextualize the sending out of the twelve and the variations in its portrayal across the Gospels.

4. Theological Significance of Discipleship: The sending out of the twelve carries profound theological significance for Christian discipleship. It underscores Jesus' authority to commission His followers and extend His ministry through them. The obedience and faithfulness of the disciples in carrying out Jesus' instructions serve as a model for believers throughout history. The variations in the Gospel accounts provide diverse perspectives on the nature and implications of discipleship.

5. Harmonization and Synoptic Relationships:

Some scholars employ harmonization techniques to reconcile the differences between Matthew, Mark, and Luke's accounts of the sending out of the twelve. They may propose harmonizing the details by considering each Gospel's unique perspective while recognizing the core message and events shared among them. Additionally, scholars explore the synoptic relationships between the Gospels, examining how the writers may have used common sources and adapted them to their theological agendas.

6. Theological Unity Amidst Diversity: Ultimately, theologians and apologists emphasize the theological unity underlying the variations in the Gospel accounts. While the details of the sending out of the twelve may differ, the overarching message of Jesus' commissioning of His disciples to proclaim the kingdom of God and heal the sick remains consistent. The diversity of perspectives enriches our understanding of Jesus' ministry and discipleship, reflecting the multifaceted nature of God's revelation in Scripture.

Expanding on these insights from scholars, theologians, and apologists provides a comprehensive framework for reconciling apparent contradictions in the details of Jesus' sending out of the twelve disciples. By considering literary, historical, cultural, and theological factors, we gain a deeper appreciation for the richness and complexity of the Gospel narratives and their implications for Christian faith and discipleship.

Summary and Reflection:

While there are differences in the details of the sending out of the twelve as recorded in Matthew 10, Mark 6, and Luke 9, the overarching message remains consistent: Jesus commissions His disciples to proclaim the kingdom of God, heal the sick, and cast out demons. The variations in the accounts highlight the diversity of perspectives and emphases within the synoptic Gospels, enriching our understanding of Jesus' ministry and the mission of His disciples.

46. The Number 144,000

Scripture References:

- Revelation 7:4-8

Analysis

The supposed contradiction regarding the number 144,000 in Revelation centers on its literal interpretation. Here's a breakdown of the issue:

Revelation 7:4-8

This passage mentions 144,000 sealed from each of the twelve tribes of Israel, totaling 144,000.

Revelation 14:1-3

This describes "a multitude that no one could count, from every nation, tribe, people and language" standing with the Lamb on Mount Zion.

The contradiction arises because:

Literal vs. Symbolic:

If 144,000 is a literal number for the Israelites, it seems like a small number compared to the "multitude from every nation" mentioned later.

Content:

The passage in Revelation 7:4-8 describes the sealing of 144,000 individuals from the twelve tribes of Israel, 12,000 from each tribe. This number has been a subject of much debate and speculation among theologians and scholars throughout history.

Language:

The language used in Revelation 7 employs symbolic imagery and apocalyptic language, which is characteristic of the genre. The description of the 144,000 sealed individuals may be interpreted symbolically, representing a complete and faithful remnant of God's people rather than a literal headcount.

Historical Background:

Understanding the historical and cultural context of the book of Revelation is crucial in interpreting its symbolism and imagery. The book was written during a time of intense persecution of Christians under the Roman

Empire, and its imagery reflects the struggles and triumphs of the early Christian community.

Theological Considerations:

From a theological perspective, the number 144,000 may symbolize completeness, perfection, or a faithful remnant of God's people. Some interpretations view the 144,000 as representative of the entire redeemed community, encompassing believers from every nation, tribe, and tongue.

Insights from Scholars, Theologians, and Apologists

<u>Various Interpretations and Perspectives:</u>

1. Symbolic Representation: Many scholars and theologians interpret the 144,000 sealed individuals symbolically rather than literally. They argue that the book of Revelation is rich in symbolic imagery, and numbers often carry symbolic significance. In this view, the number 144,000 represents completeness and perfection, symbolizing the entirety of God's redeemed people throughout history. This interpretation aligns with the broader themes of Revelation, which emphasize the victory of Christ and the ultimate triumph of God's kingdom.

2. Apocalyptic Literature: Scholars point out that Revelation belongs to the genre of apocalyptic literature, which is characterized by its use of vivid imagery, symbolism, and cosmic themes. Apocalyptic texts, including Revelation, often employ exaggerated numbers and symbolic language to convey spiritual truths and convey messages of hope and encouragement to persecuted believers. Therefore, interpreting the 144,000 sealed individuals as a literal headcount may overlook the symbolic nature of the text and its intended message.

3. Historical Context: Understanding the historical context of Revelation is essential for interpreting its symbolism and imagery accurately. The book was written during a time of intense persecution of Christians under the Roman Empire, and its imagery reflects the struggles and triumphs of the early Christian community. Many scholars argue that the sealing of the 144,000 represents God's protection and preservation of His faithful people in the face of persecution and adversity.

4. Continuity with Old Testament Imagery: Some scholars draw connections between the imagery of the 144,000 sealed individuals in Revelation and similar imagery found in the Old Testament. For example,

the idea of a faithful remnant being sealed by God is reminiscent of passages in the Old Testament prophets, such as Isaiah and Ezekiel. In this view, the 144,000 symbolize the faithful remnant of Israel who remain loyal to God amid apostasy and persecution.

5. Universal Application: While the language of Revelation 7 may initially appear to refer exclusively to a specific group of Jewish believers, many theologians argue for a broader, more inclusive interpretation. They suggest that the imagery of the 144,000 sealed individuals represents the entire redeemed community of believers, encompassing both Jews and Gentiles who have been saved by faith in Jesus Christ. This interpretation highlights the universal scope of God's redemptive plan and His desire to gather people from every nation, tribe, and tongue into His kingdom.

6. Theological Significance: Regardless of one's interpretation of the 144,000, theologians emphasize the theological significance of the passage. It underscores God's sovereignty, faithfulness, and provision for His people, even in the midst of tribulation and persecution. The imagery of the sealed individuals serves to reassure believers of God's ultimate victory over evil and His promise of salvation to all who trust in Him.

7. Diversity of Interpretation: It's essential to recognize that interpretations of the 144,000 vary among scholars, theologians, and denominations. While some adhere to a literal interpretation based on the text's explicit description, others favor a symbolic interpretation that emphasizes the broader theological themes of Revelation. The diversity of interpretations reflects the complexity of the text and the richness of its symbolism, inviting ongoing dialogue and exploration among believers.

Summary and Reflection:

The interpretation of the 144,000 sealed individuals in Revelation is a complex and multifaceted issue that has sparked much debate and discussion within Christian theology. While some interpret the passage literally, others view it symbolically, emphasizing its broader theological significance. Regardless of one's interpretation, the imagery of the 144,000 serves to convey themes of redemption, faithfulness, and the ultimate victory of God's kingdom.

47. Jesus' Anointing

Scripture References:
- Matthew 26:6-13
- Mark 14:3-9
- Luke 7:36-50
- John 12:1-8

Analysis

The supposed contradiction here concerns the anointing of Jesus with fragrant oil. There seem to be discrepancies in the details across four different Gospel accounts:

<u>Matthew 26:6-13 & Mark 14:3-9</u>: These passages describe a woman anointing Jesus' head with fragrant oil at a dinner in Bethany at the house of Simon the leper. The disciples are displeased, but Jesus defends the woman, saying she has prepared him for his burial.

<u>Luke 7:36-50</u> : Here, a sinful woman anoints Jesus' feet with tears and wipes them with her hair at a Pharisee's house named Simon. Jesus forgives her sins based on her faith and love. There's no mention of the oil being for his burial.

<u>John 12:1-8</u> : John describes Mary, the sister of Lazarus, anointing Jesus' feet with fragrant oil at a dinner in Bethany at the house of Simon the leper (potentially Lazarus himself). Judas criticizes the waste, but Jesus again defends the woman.

The contradictions seem to be:

- Number of Anointings: Was there one anointing, or two separate events?
- Location: Where did the anointing take place? Some say Bethany, others a Pharisee's house.
- Woman's Identity: Is it the same woman in all accounts, or are there different women?
- Purpose of Anointing: Was it for Jesus' burial or a gesture of love and forgiveness?

Context:

The Gospels of Matthew, Mark, Luke, and John each contain an account of Jesus being anointed, but the details surrounding the event vary between the narratives. These differences have led some to question the consistency of the accounts.

In Matthew 26 and Mark 14, the anointing occurs at the house of Simon the leper in Bethany. A woman pours expensive ointment on Jesus' head, prompting criticism from some of the disciples. Jesus defends the woman, commending her act as a preparation for His burial.

In Luke 7, the anointing takes place in the house of a Pharisee named Simon in Galilee. Here, a sinful woman enters the house and anoints Jesus' feet with ointment, washing them with her tears and drying them with her hair. Jesus forgives her sins and commends her faith.

John 12 provides another account of the anointing, which also takes place in Bethany. Here, Mary, the sister of Lazarus, anoints Jesus' feet with expensive ointment and wipes them with her hair. Judas Iscariot criticizes the act, questioning the wastefulness of the expensive ointment.

Language:

While the basic elements of the anointing are consistent across the accounts, there are variations in the specific details and the language used to describe the event. Each Gospel writer presents the story from their unique perspective, focusing on different aspects that align with their thematic goals and theological emphases.

Historical Background:

Understanding the cultural context of anointing in the ancient Near East provides insight into the significance of the event. Anointing was a common practice for guests at a meal, symbolizing hospitality, honor, and respect. The act of anointing Jesus can be interpreted as an expression of reverence and devotion by the individuals involved.

Theological Considerations:

The anointing of Jesus holds theological significance in each Gospel account. It foreshadows His impending death and burial, highlighting the sacrificial nature of His mission. The response of Jesus and those present underscores themes of forgiveness, faith, and the extravagant love of God.

Insights from Scholars, Theologians, and Apologists

<u>Various Interpretations and Perspectives:</u>

1. Literary and Theological Perspectives: Scholars often approach the differences in the Gospel accounts of Jesus' anointing from literary and theological perspectives. They recognize that each Gospel writer had a unique audience, purpose, and theological emphasis in mind when composing their narrative. Therefore, variations in details and emphasis are expected as each writer tailored their account to convey specific theological themes to their audience.

2. Multiple Anointings or Singular Event: One perspective posits that there may have been multiple anointing events involving Jesus during His ministry, each with its unique circumstances and participants. This view suggests that while the core event of anointing Jesus with expensive ointment remains consistent, different Gospel writers may have focused on different occasions or aspects of the event in their narratives.

3. Symbolism and Theological Significance: The anointing of Jesus carries profound symbolic and theological significance in each Gospel account. Scholars highlight the symbolism of the anointing as a preparation for Jesus' impending death and burial. It symbolizes honor, devotion, and recognition of Jesus' divine identity and mission. Despite variations in the details, the overarching theological message of Jesus' sacrificial death and the extravagant love of God is evident in each narrative.

4. Cultural and Historical Context: Understanding the cultural and historical context of anointing practices in the ancient Near East provides valuable insight into the significance of the event. Anointing was a common practice to honor guests and show hospitality. Therefore, the act of anointing Jesus with expensive ointment can be interpreted as an expression of reverence, devotion, and recognition of His significance.

5. The Role of Women in the Gospel Narratives: Some scholars emphasize the significant role of women in the Gospel narratives of Jesus' anointing. In Luke's account, the woman who anoints Jesus is described as a sinful woman, highlighting Jesus' compassion and willingness to extend forgiveness to those who repent. In John's Gospel, Mary, the sister of Lazarus, is depicted as the one

who anoints Jesus, underscoring her close relationship with Jesus and her act of extravagant love and devotion.

6. Theological Unity Amidst Diversity: Despite the variations and differences in the Gospel accounts of Jesus' anointing, scholars emphasize the theological unity that underlies these narratives. The core message of Jesus' sacrificial death, the forgiveness of sins, and the expression of extravagant love remains consistent across the Gospels, illustrating the diverse perspectives and experiences of those who encountered Jesus during His earthly ministry.

7. Encouragement for Further Reflection: Scholars, theologians, and apologists encourage believers to engage in further reflection and study of the Gospel accounts of Jesus' anointing. These narratives invite readers to explore the profound theological truths and themes embedded within the text and to deepen their understanding of Jesus' identity, mission, and significance in salvation history.

Summary and Reflection:

Despite variations in the accounts of Jesus' anointing in Matthew 26, Mark 14, Luke 7, and John 12, the core themes of devotion, sacrifice, and the impending death of Jesus shine through. Each Gospel writer presents the event from their unique perspective, highlighting different aspects of the story that contribute to the richness and depth of the Gospel message. Ultimately, the diverse accounts of Jesus' anointing invite readers to reflect on the profound love and devotion expressed by those who encountered Him during His earthly ministry.

48. Paul's First Visit to Jerusalem

Scripture References:
- Acts 9:26-30
- Galatians 1:18-19

<u>Analysis</u>

The supposed contradiction here concerns Paul's (formerly Saul) first visit to Jerusalem after his conversion. Here's the breakdown:

<u>Acts 9:26-30</u>

This passage describes Paul going to Jerusalem after his conversion in Damascus. He tries to join the disciples, but they are afraid of him. Barnabas intervenes and vouches for Paul, who then spends fifteen days with Cephas (Peter) and sees no other apostles.

<u>Galatians 1:17-20</u>

Paul, in his letter to the Galatians, states he went to Arabia after his conversion and then returned to Damascus. Only three years later did he go to Jerusalem to visit Cephas (Peter) for fifteen days, and he saw no other apostles except James, the Lord's brother.

The contradiction seems to be:

- Timing: Acts suggests an immediate visit to Jerusalem, while Galatians implies a three-year gap.
- Contact with Apostles: Acts mentions spending time with "the apostles," while Galatians clarifies only seeing Peter and James.

Context:

In Acts 9, Luke provides a narrative account of Paul's conversion on the road to Damascus and his subsequent activities, including his visit to Jerusalem. The focus is on Paul's interaction with the disciples in Jerusalem and the initial skepticism they have towards him due to his past persecution of Christians.

In Galatians 1, Paul provides a personal testimony of his conversion and early ministry, including his visit to Jerusalem. He emphasizes that his knowledge of the gospel did not come from human sources but through direct revelation from Jesus Christ. Paul's purpose in recounting his visit to Jerusalem is to establish his independence as an apostle and the authenticity of his message.

Harmonization Attempts:

Some scholars propose harmonization attempts to reconcile the apparent discrepancy between Acts 9 and Galatians 1. They suggest that Paul's encounter with Peter and James mentioned in Galatians 1:18-19 may have occurred separately from his interaction with the disciples described in Acts 9:26-30. Additionally, it is possible that Paul's brief encounter with Peter and James did not involve a formal meeting with the entire group of apostles.

Theological Significance:

The discrepancy between Acts 9 and Galatians 1 regarding Paul's first visit to Jerusalem does not significantly impact the theological message of the New Testament. Both accounts emphasize Paul's conversion experience and his subsequent ministry, highlighting the transformative power of encountering the risen Christ and the calling to proclaim the gospel to both Jews and Gentiles.

Insights from Scholars, Theologians, and Apologists

Various Interpretations and Perspectives:

1. Historical and Contextual Analysis: Scholars often conduct a detailed examination of the historical and contextual factors surrounding Paul's first visit to Jerusalem. They consider the cultural dynamics, the socio-political landscape of the time, and the nuances of early Christian communities. By delving into the historical context, scholars aim to gain a deeper understanding of the events described in Acts 9 and Galatians 1, which can shed light on any apparent contradictions.

2. Literary and Genre Considerations: The differences between Acts and Galatians in their portrayal of Paul's first visit to Jerusalem may also be approached from a literary and genre perspective. Scholars analyze the distinct purposes and literary conventions of these texts. Acts, for instance, is a historical narrative written by Luke, while Galatians is a letter penned by Paul. Understanding the genre and literary conventions of each text can provide insights into their respective portrayals of events.

3. Theological Implications: Theological considerations play a significant role in reconciling apparent contradictions in biblical texts. Scholars and theologians explore the theological themes and motifs present in Acts and

Galatians, considering how these texts contribute to the overarching theological narrative of the New Testament. The focus shifts from mere chronological accuracy to the theological truths conveyed through Paul's conversion and ministry.

4. Harmonization Attempts: Some scholars propose harmonization attempts to reconcile the differences between Acts 9 and Galatians 1 regarding Paul's first visit to Jerusalem. They suggest plausible scenarios where Paul's encounters with Peter and James in Galatians 1 may have occurred separately from his interactions with the disciples in Acts 9. By harmonizing the accounts, scholars aim to present a coherent narrative that aligns with the broader theological themes of the New Testament.

5. The Reliability of Scripture: Apologists often emphasize the reliability of Scripture despite apparent contradictions or discrepancies. They highlight the diverse perspectives and voices present in the biblical texts, viewing them as complementary rather than contradictory. Apologists argue that differences in details or emphasis do not undermine the overall reliability or truthfulness of the biblical accounts. Instead, they affirm the rich tapestry of Scripture, which reflects the complexity of human experiences and encounters with God.

6. Encouraging Further Study: Scholars, theologians, and apologists encourage further study and reflection on passages like Paul's first visit to Jerusalem. They invite readers to engage critically with the biblical text, considering its historical, literary, and theological dimensions. By embracing a posture of intellectual curiosity and openness, individuals can deepen their understanding of Scripture and grow in their faith.

7. The Mystery of Divine Revelation: Ultimately, scholars, theologians, and apologists acknowledge the mystery of divine revelation in Scripture. They recognize that human authors, inspired by the Holy Spirit, wrote from their unique perspectives and experiences. As such, apparent contradictions or discrepancies may serve to highlight the multifaceted nature of divine truth and the limitations of human understanding. Rather than discouraging exploration, these complexities invite deeper contemplation and reliance on God's wisdom.

Summary and Reflection:

While there may be discrepancies between Acts 9 and Galatians 1 regarding Paul's first visit to Jerusalem after his conversion, the overarching theological message of Paul's encounter with the risen Christ and his subsequent ministry remains consistent. These accounts invite readers to reflect on the transformative power of God's

49. Portrayal of Wisdom

Scripture References:
- Proverbs 4:5-7 (NIV)
- Ecclesiastes 7:19 (NIV)
- Matthew 11:25-26 (NIV)

<u>Analysis</u>

The supposed contradiction here seems to be that Proverbs and Ecclesiastes praise wisdom as valuable and powerful, while Matthew portrays Jesus saying God hides things from the "wise and understanding." Let's delve deeper:

Similarities:

- All these passages ultimately acknowledge God's role. Even in Proverbs and Ecclesiastes, where the value of wisdom is emphasised, obtaining it might involve seeking God's guidance.

Differences:

- Focus: Proverbs and Ecclesiastes focus on the practical benefits of wisdom in this life. Matthew emphasizes spiritual understanding and receptivity to God's message.

- Type of Wisdom: Proverbs and Ecclesiastes might refer to a broader concept of wisdom, including knowledge and good judgment. Matthew might be referring to a more specific type of spiritual understanding that comes from God's revelation.

Context:

The verses from Proverbs, Ecclesiastes, and Matthew present varying perspectives on the nature and value of wisdom. Proverbs extols the virtues of wisdom, equating it with life and beauty. Ecclesiastes emphasizes the power of wisdom to strengthen the wise. However, Matthew presents a seemingly contrasting view, where Jesus expresses gratitude that certain truths are hidden from the wise and understanding.

Proverbs 4:5-7 encourages the pursuit and retention of wisdom, depicting it as essential for life and an adornment of beauty. It emphasizes the importance of not forgetting or turning away from the wisdom imparted.

Ecclesiastes 7:19 underscores the potency of wisdom, stating that it strengthens the wise even more than ten rulers of a city. Here, wisdom is portrayed as a powerful asset that enhances one's ability to navigate life effectively.

In Matthew 11:25-26, Jesus expresses gratitude to God for concealing certain truths from the wise and understanding while revealing them to "little children." This passage seems to contrast with the previous verses by suggesting that wisdom is not always synonymous with understanding or intellectual prowess.

Language:

The language used in Proverbs and Ecclesiastes elevates wisdom as a highly valuable and desirable attribute. It employs imagery and metaphors to illustrate the benefits and potency of wisdom. In contrast, the language in Matthew's passage highlights the humility and simplicity associated with those to whom God reveals truths.

Historical Background:

Understanding the historical context of each book sheds light on the portrayal of wisdom. Proverbs and Ecclesiastes are part of the wisdom literature in the Old Testament, which often extols the virtues of wisdom and its practical benefits. Matthew, on the other hand, records Jesus' teachings during His earthly ministry, which often challenged conventional wisdom and highlighted the importance of humility and childlike faith.

Theological Considerations:

The apparent contradiction reflects different aspects of wisdom and understanding within the broader theological framework. While Proverbs and Ecclesiastes emphasize the value and potency of wisdom in practical living, Matthew's passage highlights the limitations of human wisdom and the importance of spiritual receptivity and humility.

Insights from Scholars, Theologians, and Apologists

<u>Various Interpretations and Perspectives:</u>

1. Contextual Understanding: Scholars emphasize the importance of understanding the cultural and historical context of each passage. Proverbs and Ecclesiastes, as part of the wisdom literature in the Old Testament, present wisdom in a practical and earthly context. In contrast, Matthew's Gospel records Jesus' teachings, often challenging conventional wisdom and highlighting spiritual truths.

2. Multifaceted Nature of Wisdom: Theological experts highlight the multifaceted nature of wisdom presented in Scripture. While Proverbs and Ecclesiastes emphasize the practical benefits of wisdom in daily living and decision-making, Matthew's passage underscores the superiority of spiritual wisdom over human understanding. This nuanced understanding allows for a harmonious interpretation of the diverse perspectives on wisdom.

3. Spiritual Discernment and Humility: Apologists stress the importance of spiritual discernment and humility in interpreting these passages. While earthly wisdom may have its value, spiritual wisdom—revealed by God and accessible to those with childlike faith—surpasses human understanding. This perspective aligns with Jesus' teachings on humility and receptivity to divine revelation.

4. Integration of Perspectives: Scholars advocate for an integrated approach to understanding wisdom, drawing insights from Proverbs, Ecclesiastes, and Matthew. Rather than viewing the passages in isolation, they suggest synthesizing the diverse perspectives to gain a comprehensive understanding of wisdom's significance in both practical and spiritual realms.

5. Application to Life: Theological reflections on these passages extend beyond academic discourse to practical application in daily life. Understanding the multifaceted nature of wisdom enables believers to navigate life's complexities with humility, discernment, and a reliance on God's guidance. By integrating the practical wisdom of Proverbs and Ecclesiastes with the spiritual insights of Matthew, individuals can cultivate a holistic approach to wisdom that enriches their relationship with God and others.

6. Continued Study and Reflection: Scholars encourage continued study and reflection on these passages, recognizing that the pursuit of wisdom is a lifelong journey. Engaging with Scripture with an open mind and a humble heart allows believers to glean new insights and deepen their understanding of God's wisdom revealed through His Word.

Summary and Reflection:

While there may appear to be a contradiction in the portrayal of wisdom in Proverbs, Ecclesiastes, and Matthew, a closer examination reveals complementary perspectives on the multifaceted nature of wisdom. Each passage offers valuable insights into the significance of wisdom in practical living, spiritual discernment, and humility before God. Ultimately, these passages invite readers to seek wisdom with a humble and receptive heart, recognizing its transformative power in all aspects of life.

True wisdom encompasses both practical discernment and spiritual insight, ultimately leading to a deeper understanding of God and His purposes. As believers seek wisdom, they are called to embrace humility, childlike faith, and a reliance on God's guidance, recognizing that true wisdom comes from above.

50. Jesus' Last Words

Scripture References:

- Matthew 27:46
- Mark 15:34
- Luke 23:46
- John 19:30

Analysis:

There isn't one universally agreed-upon contradiction regarding Jesus' last words, but there are variations in how the Gospels depict them (Matthew 27:46, Mark 15:34, Luke 23:46, John 19:30). Here's a breakdown:

* Matthew: "My God, my God, why have you forsaken me?" (This reflects a quote from Psalm 22:1)

* Mark: "Eloi, Eloi, lema sabachthani?" (This is an Aramaic phrase with a similar meaning to Matthew's quote)

* Luke: "Father, into your hands I commend my spirit."

* John: "It is finished."

Context:

The Gospels record different statements attributed to Jesus as His last words on the cross. Matthew and Mark both mention Jesus crying out, "My God, my God, why have you forsaken me?" Luke records Jesus saying, "Father, into your hands I commit my spirit," while John records, "It is finished."

Each Gospel writer emphasizes different aspects of Jesus' final moments on the cross, reflecting their unique theological perspectives and the intended audiences of their writings. While the words vary, they collectively convey the significance of Jesus' sacrificial death and the fulfillment of His mission.

Language:

The language used in each Gospel passage reflects the theological themes and literary styles of the respective writers. Matthew and Mark's accounts highlight Jesus' sense of abandonment, echoing Psalm 22:1, while Luke emphasizes Jesus' trust in the Father and His voluntary surrender. John's statement emphasizes the completion of Jesus' redemptive work.

Historical Background:

Understanding the historical and cultural context of crucifixion in Roman Palestine helps interpret Jesus' last words. Crucifixion was a brutal form of execution, and individuals often experienced intense physical and emotional suffering. Jesus' words reflect His humanity and the profound spiritual anguish He endured.

Theological Considerations:

The various statements attributed to Jesus at the cross highlight different theological aspects of His redemptive work. Matthew and Mark's accounts emphasize Jesus' identification with human suffering and His role as the fulfillment of Messianic prophecy. Luke's account underscores Jesus' trust in the Father's sovereignty and His willingness to surrender His life. John's statement emphasizes the accomplishment of salvation through Jesus' sacrificial death.

Insights from Scholars, Theologians, and Apologists Various Interpretations and Perspectives:

1. Theological Significance: Scholars emphasize the theological depth embedded in Jesus' last words. Each statement reflects different aspects of Jesus' redemptive work and the profound implications of His sacrificial death for humanity's salvation. The variations among the Gospel accounts highlight the multifaceted nature of Jesus' mission and the richness of theological reflection on His crucifixion.

2. Christological Reflection: Theologians delve into the Christological implications of Jesus' last words. They explore how each statement reveals unique aspects of Jesus' identity as the divine Son of God and the suffering Messiah. Through these words, Jesus demonstrates His solidarity with human suffering while also expressing His trust in the Father's plan for redemption.

3. Narrative Function: Apologists consider the narrative function of Jesus' last words within each Gospel account. They highlight how each Gospel writer selects and presents Jesus' final utterances to serve the overarching theological themes and literary purposes of their respective narratives. While the words may vary, they collectively contribute to the cohesive portrayal of Jesus' mission and message.

4. Historical Authenticity: Scholars analyze the historical authenticity of Jesus' last words, taking into account factors such as eyewitness testimony, textual variants, and cultural context. While some differences may arise due to translation or transmission issues, scholars affirm the general reliability of the Gospel accounts in preserving the core message of Jesus' crucifixion and resurrection.

5. Harmonization Attempts: Some scholars propose harmonization techniques to reconcile the variations among the Gospel accounts of Jesus' last words. They suggest plausible scenarios in which Jesus may have spoken multiple statements during His crucifixion, with each Gospel writer selecting the one most relevant to their theological emphasis or narrative focus.

6. Devotional Reflection: Theological scholars and apologists encourage devotional reflection on Jesus' last words as a means of deepening one's faith and understanding of the Christian message. They invite believers to meditate on the significance of Jesus' sacrifice and the assurance of salvation conveyed through His final utterances.

Summary and Reflection:

While the Gospels record different statements as Jesus' last words on the cross, these variations do not constitute a contradiction but rather offer complementary perspectives on the significance of Jesus' death and resurrection. Together, they affirm the central message of the Gospel—that through His sacrificial death, Jesus accomplished salvation for humanity and ushered in the kingdom of God.

Chapter 5: Faith in Biblical Interpretation

- The Nature of Faith
- Faith as a Foundation for Interpretation
- Faith and the Interpretation of Difficult Passages
- Faith and Hermeneutics
- Faith and Personal Revelation
- Faith and Personal Revelation

Introduction to Faith in Biblical Interpretation:

Interpreting the Bible goes beyond mere intellectual exercise; it involves a deep spiritual journey guided by faith.

The Nature of Faith:

Faith is not merely believing in something without evidence; it is a dynamic and transformative trust in God and His Word. It involves intellectual assent, heartfelt conviction, and active obedience. Understanding the nature of faith is essential for grasping its role in biblical interpretation.

Faith as a Foundation for Interpretation:

Faith serves as the bedrock upon which our interpretation of Scripture is built. It shapes our worldview, values, and presuppositions, influencing how we approach and understand the text. Our belief in the reliability and authority of God's Word informs and guides our interpretation.

Faith and the Interpretation of Difficult Passages:

When confronted with difficult or challenging passages in Scripture, faith enables us to grapple with ambiguity and uncertainty. Our trust in God's wisdom and goodness empowers us to seek understanding even in the midst of apparent contradictions or complexities. Faith prompts us to approach difficult passages with humility and openness to divine guidance.

Faith and Hermeneutics:

Hermeneutics, the principles and methods of biblical interpretation, are deeply intertwined with faith. Our beliefs about the nature of Scripture, the character of God, and the work of the Holy Spirit shape our interpretive approach. Faith informs how we apply hermeneutical principles and guides us in discerning the intended meaning of the text.

Faith and Personal Revelation:

Faith opens the door to personal revelation and illumination as we engage with Scripture. It is through faith that we encounter God's truth in a transformative way, leading to deeper insights and spiritual growth. Our trust in God's Spirit enables us to discern His voice and receive fresh understanding and application of His Word.

Conclusion: Embracing Faith in Biblical Interpretation:

In conclusion, embracing faith as an integral aspect of biblical interpretation is essential for a robust and meaningful engagement with Scripture. As we journey through the pages of the Bible, let us approach God's Word with humility, trust, and a willingness to allow faith to guide our understanding and application. May our study of Scripture be characterized by a deepening reliance on God and a growing receptivity to His truth revealed through His Word.

Chapter 6: Allowing Guidance of the Holy Spirit

- The Nature and Work of the Holy Spirit
- Preparing the Heart and Mind for Spiritual Guidance
- Faith and Trust in the Holy Spirit
- Listening to the Voice of the Holy Spirit
- Walking in Step with the Holy Spirit
- Obstacles to Spirit-Led Living
- Embracing Spirit-Led Living

Understanding the Role of the Holy Spirit

When we embark on a journey through the boundless depths and infinite treasures of the Bible. We will realize that scripture is not merely a collection of ancient texts but a living, breathing testimony of God's eternal truth and unchanging love for humanity. As we delve into the pages of the Bible, we discover a wealth of wisdom, guidance, and revelation that has the power to transform our lives and draw us closer to God.

The Nature and Work of the Holy Spirit

Central to our exploration of Scripture is an understanding of the role of the Holy Spirit. The Holy Spirit, often referred to as the Spirit of Truth, is the divine agent who inspired the writing of Scripture and continues to illuminate its truths to believers. As Jesus promised, the Holy Spirit guides us into all truth, enabling us to discern the deeper meanings and applications of God's Word in our lives.

Preparing the Heart and Mind for Spiritual Guidance

Before delving into the study of Scripture, it is essential to prepare our hearts and minds for spiritual guidance. This involves cultivating a receptive attitude and a posture of humility before God. Scripture teaches us that those who approach God's Word with a pure heart and a humble spirit are more likely to receive illumination and understanding from the Holy Spirit.

Faith and Trust in the Holy Spirit

Faith plays a crucial role in our interaction with Scripture. Without faith, it is impossible to please God or fully grasp the truths revealed in His Word. As we study Scripture, we must trust in the Holy Spirit to lead us into all truth, believing that He will illuminate our minds and hearts with divine wisdom and insight. Scripture assures us that the Holy Spirit is our Helper, Counselor, and Guide, empowering us to understand and apply God's Word in our lives.

Listening to the Voice of the Holy Spirit

The Holy Spirit speaks to us through Scripture, prompting us to delve deeper into its truths and guiding us in our interpretation and application of God's Word. As we spend time in prayer and meditation on Scripture, we open ourselves up to the leading of the Holy Spirit, allowing Him to speak to us personally and reveal His will for our lives.

Walking in Step with the Holy Spirit

Living a Spirit-led life requires surrendering our will and desires to the leading of the Holy Spirit. This involves aligning our thoughts, words, and actions with the principles and values revealed in Scripture. The Holy Spirit empowers us to walk in obedience to God's Word, enabling us to live lives that are pleasing to Him and bear witness to His grace and truth.

Obstacles to Spirit-Led Living

While the Holy Spirit is ever-present and willing to guide us, there are obstacles that can hinder our receptivity to His leading. These may include pride, self-reliance, and spiritual resistance. By acknowledging these barriers and seeking the Holy Spirit's help, we can overcome them and experience the fullness of Spirit-led living.

Conclusion: Embracing Spirit-Led Living

In conclusion, the guidance of the Holy Spirit is indispensable in our study and interpretation of Scripture. By relying on the Holy Spirit to lead us into all truth, we can navigate the complexities of Scripture with confidence and discernment. Let us embrace the leading of the Holy Spirit in our study of God's Word, trusting in His wisdom and guidance to illuminate its truths and transform our lives. As we yield to the Holy Spirit's leading, may we grow in our understanding of Scripture, deepen our relationship with God, and be empowered to live lives that honor and glorify Him.

Chapter 7: Never Stop Studying the Bible

- The Endless Riches of Scripture
- The Eternal Relevance of God's Word
- Cultivating a Lifelong Habit of Bible Study
- Deepening Understanding Through Study Methods
- Engaging with Scripture in Community
- Applying Scripture to Everyday Life
- Embracing the Journey of Lifelong Learning

The Endless Riches of Scripture

In the vast expanse of human history, few texts have endured the test of time and remained as relevant and transformative as the Bible. Its pages are not mere words but a living testimony to the enduring love, wisdom, and truth of God. As believers, we are privileged to have access to this divine revelation, a guidebook for life, a source of comfort in trials, and a beacon of hope in times of darkness.

The Eternal Relevance of God's Word

The timeless nature of Scripture is evident in its ability to speak to the deepest longings of the human heart, transcending cultural and temporal boundaries. From Genesis to Revelation, its narratives, teachings, and prophecies resonate with the universal human experience, offering solace, guidance, and direction to all who heed its call.

Embedded within its pages are truths that withstand the test of time, principles that shape our character, and promises that anchor our faith. As Isaiah declares, "The grass withers, the flower fades, but the word of our God will stand forever" (Isaiah 40:8). In a world marked by uncertainty and change, the unchanging Word of God serves as a steadfast anchor for our souls.

Cultivating a Lifelong Habit of Bible Study

To fully harness the transformative power of Scripture, we must cultivate a lifelong habit of Bible study. Just as physical nourishment sustains our bodies, regular engagement with God's Word nourishes our souls, strengthening our faith and fortifying our spirits for the journey ahead.

The psalmist declares, "Your word is a lamp to my feet and a light to my path" (Psalm 119:105). Through diligent study and meditation, we gain insight into God's will for our lives, discern His voice amidst the noise of the world, and find direction for every step we take.

Deepening Understanding Through Study Methods

Delving deeper into Scripture requires more than passive reading; it demands active engagement and discernment. By employing various study methods and techniques, such as historical context, literary analysis, and thematic study, we uncover layers of meaning and uncover hidden treasures within its pages.

As Paul exhorts Timothy, "Do your best to present yourself to God as one approved, a worker who has no need to be ashamed, rightly handling the word of truth" (2 Timothy 2:15). Through diligent study and application of biblical principles, we equip ourselves to navigate life's challenges with wisdom and discernment.

Engaging with Scripture in Community

While personal study is essential, engaging with Scripture in community adds depth and richness to our understanding. Through group Bible studies, discipleship relationships, and corporate worship, we benefit from the collective wisdom and encouragement of fellow believers.

Hebrews reminds us, "And let us consider how to stir up one another to love and good works, not neglecting to meet together, as is the habit of some, but encouraging one another, and all the more as you see the Day drawing near" (Hebrews 10:24-25). In the fellowship of believers, we find strength, accountability, and mutual edification as we journey together in faith.

Applying Scripture to Everyday Life

Ultimately, the goal of Bible study is not merely intellectual comprehension but practical application. James admonishes us, "But be doers of the word, and not hearers only, deceiving yourselves" (James 1:22). As we apply God's Word to our everyday lives, we experience transformation, renewal, and empowerment for righteous living.

Whether in times of joy or sorrow, triumph or tribulation, the Word of God serves as our guide, our comfort, and our source of strength. By allowing its truths to penetrate our hearts and minds, we become vessels of His grace, reflecting His love and light to a world in need.

Embracing the Journey of Lifelong Learning

In conclusion, the journey of studying the Bible is not a destination but a lifelong pursuit. As we delve deeper into its truths, we discover afresh the beauty, complexity, and majesty of God's Word. Let us, therefore, commit ourselves to never stop studying the Bible, knowing that in its pages, we find wisdom for the present, hope for the future, and the revelation of God's unfailing love.

Conclusion:

Final Thoughts on the Consistency and Reliability of Scripture:

As we draw near the conclusion of our journey through the pages of Scripture, it becomes abundantly clear that the Word of God is not only consistent but also remarkably reliable in its message and teachings. Despite the diversity of its authors, the span of centuries over which it was written, and the varied cultural contexts in which its books originated, the Bible maintains a remarkable unity of purpose and theme.

From Genesis to Revelation, its narratives, prophecies, and teachings harmonize to form a cohesive and coherent testimony to the character and purposes of God. Its central message of redemption through Christ, the overarching narrative of creation, fall, and restoration, and the timeless principles of love, justice, and mercy woven throughout its pages attest to its divine origin and inspiration.

The apparent discrepancies and challenges encountered in Scripture serve not as evidence of its unreliability but rather as opportunities for deeper exploration and understanding. Through diligent study, prayerful reflection, and the illumination of the Holy Spirit, we discover that what may seem like contradictions are often invitations to delve deeper into the riches of God's Word, uncovering layers of meaning and truth that enrich our faith and transform our lives.

In the face of skepticism and criticism, the consistency and reliability of Scripture stand as a testament to its divine authorship and enduring relevance. As Peter affirms, "For no prophecy was ever produced by the will of man, but men spoke from God as they were carried along by the Holy Spirit" (2 Peter 1:21). The Word of God transcends human limitations and remains an unchanging standard of truth and righteousness in a world marked by uncertainty and moral relativism.

Therefore, let us approach the study and interpretation of Scripture with humility, reverence, and a firm conviction in its infallibility. Let us trust in the faithfulness of God to preserve His Word throughout the ages, knowing that His truth endures forever. And let us be diligent stewards of the Scriptures, allowing its life-giving message to shape our beliefs, guide our actions, and transform our hearts.

In closing, may we echo the psalmist's declaration, "The law of the Lord is perfect, reviving the soul; the testimony of the Lord is sure, making wise the simple" (Psalm 19:7). May we continue to treasure and cherish the Word of God as the ultimate source of wisdom, guidance, and truth, confident in its consistency and reliability for all eternity.

TRUTH